Administering Development
in the
Third World

Administering Development in the Third World

CONSTRAINTS AND CHOICES

Hari Mohan Mathur

SAGE PUBLICATIONS
New Delhi/Beverly Hills/London

First published in 1986 by

Sage Publications India Pvt Ltd
32, M-Block Market, Greater Kailash I
New Delhi 110 048

Sage Publications Inc **Sage Publications Ltd**
275 South Beverly Drive   28 Banner Street
Beverly Hills, California 90212   London EC1Y 8 QE, England

Published by Tejeshwar Singh for Sage Publications India Pvt Ltd
Phototypeset by Printers Plates, Madras, printed by Taj Press.

311990

Library of Congress Cataloging in Publication Data
Mathur, Hari Mohan.
  Administering development in the Third World.
  Includes index.
  1. Rural development — Developing countries.
  2. Rural development — Developing countries — Citizen participation. I. Title.
  HN981. C6M88   1986   307.1'4' 091724   86-6503
  ISBN 0-8039-9506-7 (U.S. — hbk.) ISBN 81-7036-026-9 (India — hbk.)
  ISBN 0-8039-9507-5 (U.S. — pbk.) ISBN 81-7036-027-7 (India — pbk.)

CONTENTS

Preface

Governments in most Third World countries are now actively promoting development. Their role in this sphere is no longer restricted to building infrastructure which, in turn, could stimulate growth. More and more, governments are getting directly involved in productive activities and service sectors. On the whole, the results of this activism have been beneficial to the people. However, in many countries the performance of government-administered programmes does not appear yet to be measuring up to the expectations aroused initially.

Why do plans and projects, formulated with so much care, encounter problems in implementation? What is really hampering the development effort? As numerous studies have recently brought out, the inefficiency of the administrative system is proving to be a major constraint on development. Moreover, as findings from these researches indicate the administrative capacity, which is in short supply everywhere is particularly scarce in the Third World.

The human element in development has lately acquired a new significance. Getting over their earlier obsession with economic growth per se, planners now readily appreciate that it is the happiness of man that ultimately counts. Consequently, the whole purpose of development is being redefined so as to bring people right on to the centre stage. This basic change in the meaning of development has further added new dimensions to the administrative task.

People have, in fact, mattered virtually nothing to planners and administrators all these years. Local knowledge and capacity have often been viewed disdainfully as of little avail even in matters related to simple changes in the village life. At the same time, most administrators are firmly of the view that they alone know all about development, and that only their answers to development problems are the right ones. The one role that they are willing to concede for the people is that of acting as recipients of services offered by governmental agencies set up to promote development.

The fact is that the capacity of the people to contribute to development is immense. They represent a resource for development which has remained largely untapped. People are rightly sceptical of the outsider and specially his ideas on development which, howsoever useful for a particular setting, may not necessarily be workable in their situation. Indeed, the top-down planning methods which have long been in vogue need to be substituted by methods that seek the active involvement of people in all stages of development planning, implementation, monitoring and evaluation. If development is to further enhance the capacity of the people to determine their own future, it is essential that they are drawn into development processes unhesitatingly.

Recent experience indicates that involvement of the people in decision-making concerning their development has been a decisive factor in the success of many projects. On the other hand, it is projects which do not take the people factor into account that almost invariably run into difficulties. What is even more important, confirmatory evidence in support of these propositions has come in for a variety of projects from widely divergent geographic locations.

Experts and agencies of the United Nations and the World Bank involved in promoting development in the Third World are now arguing the case for more and more participation. There is no particular philosophical slant to their concern for people-centred development. They regard participation desirable purely from considerations of a practical kind — participation has contributed to efficiencies in project designing and operations in several significant ways.

Voices supporting participatory development are also being increasingly heard in many Third World countries. At the present moment, no discussion on development seems to take place without some reference being made to people as partners in the development effort. However, participation can easily turn into a cliche, especially for those administering programmes of human development. It is one thing to laud the idea, but quite another thing to do all that is needed to translate it into reality.

In fact some people are now beginning to wonder whether official

employee

agencies and governmental functionaries are the most suitable instruments for carrying out development operations. Their capability is being questioned not because of any discernible indifference towards the poor on their part, but perhaps because of their inexperience in dealing with such problems. Indeed, people-centred development is a new concept, and the bureaucracy does not seem to be equipped yet in coping with all the emerging problems. As development programmes targeted on the poor are highly sensitive to the quality of implementation, difficulties have inevitably arisen in many cases.

Notwithstanding its shortcomings and failures, the bureaucracy is going to be entrusted with development work much more than was the case previously. Even the severest critics of bureaucracy do not suggest its abandonment. Apparently, there is no alternative to it. The growing consensus only favours further strengthening of administration in ways that turn it into an effective instrument of promoting the development process. Experience suggests that it is not easy to bring about improvements in administration. Yet it is urgent that the desired changes in administration occur speedily.

While much has been written on planning methods for development, the administrative dimension has remained largely a neglected area. It is only now in the context of a growing concern for improving the living conditions of masses in the Third World that the issues related to administration for development have begun attracting attention. This book attempts to analyse and understand just these issues. Quite obviously, the significant strands in present-day thinking alone are included in the discussion. The administrative dimension in Third World development is a subject that is vast and rapidly growing.

This overview of the emerging ideas on development, the inadequacies of the existing, still largely traditional, administrative system in coping with newer development challenges, and the methods being currently considered for adapting administration to the requirements of people-centred development, is based on papers I wrote in recent years. Working during this period as Specialist in Development Administration at the United Nations Asian and Pacific Development Centre, Kuala Lumpur, Malaysia, as Consultant to the Food and Agriculture Organization of the United Nations, Rome, and in other places, I had opportunities both to pursue my research interests and to observe first-hand development in action in many countries of Asia, Africa and Latin America. My writings clearly reflect this rich experience.

The list of colleagues who have helped to make this publication possible is rather long. They gave assistance at various stages, in different ways, by inviting me to write papers, by discussing ideas, by giving information, by providing encouragement, etc. I wish I could thank them by name, but that does not seem possible as some may indeed prefer to remain anonymous. However, this help is most gratefully acknowledged.

HARI MOHAN MATHUR

Acknowledgements

This book includes material which was originally prepared for other publications, occasions as documented below.

Chapter 1 is based on a paper prepared for the *18th SID World Conference,* Rome, 1-4 July 1985. Chapter 2 is from Hari Mohan Mathur and Helmut Palla (eds.). 1984. *Regional Development and Local Administration* Berlin: German Foundation for International Development. pp. 207-43. Chapter 3 was commissioned as a discussion paper by FAO of the UN and presented at the *Global Expert Consultation on Organization and Management Structures for Rural Development* organised by FAO in Rome, 12-15 December 1983. Chapter 4 is from Hari Mohan Mathur. 1983. *Training of Development Administrators.* Kuala Lumpur: United Nations Asian and Pacific Development Centre. pp. 3-36. Chapter 5 is based on a paper prepared for *IUAES Intercongress,* Amsterdam, April 1981. A slightly abridged version of this paper later appeared in *IFDA DOSSIER,* 27 January-February 1982, under the title 'The Role of Anthropologists in Rural Development'. Chapter 6 is from *Development Policy and Administration Review,* Vol. I, No. 2, July-December 1975, pp. 105-20. This is based on a study done at the Institute of Development Studies at the University of Sussex, Brighton.

Permission granted for reproduction of these papers is acknowledged with thanks.

Participatory Development and Public Administration

Popular participation in the development process first appeared in more developed societies. Its emergence coincided with the growth in education, the rise of democratic institutions, and the spread of communications. The opening sentence of an important study focused on political dimensions of the participation process in developing countries reads: 'Broadening political participation is a hallmark of political modernization.'[1] Evidence, longitudinal as well as cross-national, in support of this proposition is abundant. 'Traditional society,' wrote Daniel Lerner quarter of a century ago, 'is non-participant.... Modern society is participant.'[2] It is a well established fact that in developed countries more people become involved in decision-making through citizen action groups and many other ways than is the case in countries which are less developed.[3] On the other hand, government in traditional societies tends to remain the concern of a small elite group.[4]

However, the present day Third World scene does not seem to be conforming to this pattern. In fact, the entire process of development in the Third World is now perceived as dependent on participation. Poona Wignaraja emphatically states that 'It is a pretense to think that the crisis that the Third World is facing can be overcome and that the reshaping of its societies and the development of its rural areas can be undertaken without the participation of the people, particularly the large numbers who are poor.'[5]

There is a growing consensus that people everywhere have a basic human right to take part in decisions that affect their lives. Consequently, participation in Third World countries is being promoted by the United Nations agencies and the governments themselves.[6]

China, Tanzania and Guyana are among the developing countries where participation has proceeded quite far.[7] This experience suggests — and encourages the hope — that participation is possible even in societies that are not yet part of the developed world. Following the success of these efforts, participation in some form or the other is being included as an important element in development strategies of most Third World countries.[8]

People-Centred Development

People usually did not count for much in the past. Consequently, the planning methods in vogue then were unambiguously top-down: Central Government agencies decided on projects which in their view were best suited for people living in far-off villages, and notified the community concerned later only in case manual labour was needed to carry out the project work. It is little wonder that such development efforts failed to enthuse the poor, and extend the intended benefits to them.[9]

Planners are now beginning to perceive their task differently. 'Putting people first' in development projects has emerged as a major concern of planners in recent years.[10] There is a growing awareness of the fact that people cannot be ignored any more if their development is what the plans aim to promote.[11] On the goals of development, the consensus which is emerging favours for the people a central place in the whole scheme of things.[12] Statements such as the one which Cocoyoc participants adopted are readily evoking acceptance almost universally. 'The goal of development should be not to develop things, but to develop man' beautifully sums up what planners now think should be the real aim of development.[13]

In the changed situation, the development task cannot be carried on as before; it acquires a new orientation. Several factors have conspired to generate the current concern with the participation of target groups in their own development. Rogers *et al.* list three main reasons for this change in development thinking:

First, and foremost, there is a growing awareness among many developing nations that their greatest resource in the development process is their own people. A second reason is the increasing realisation by those responsible for the varied government delivery systems — agricultural extension, health and family planning field workers, among others — that the ready consumption of delivered entities is dependent upon actual demand. Third, centralized patterns of development decision-making have generally been unable to accommodate local socio-cultural variations or to mobilize needed local resources.[14]

Why Participation?

Even more than the people affected, it is the development planners who now favour participation. They want people to participate not only in sharing the fruits of development, but also in contributing to the process of development at every stage from planning to evaluation through implementation and monitoring.[15] Experience' suggests that development plans have a greater chance of success with the involvement of target groups.[16] On the contrary, planners are quite certain in their minds that without the cooperation of the people there is every likelihood of projects not proceeding along their planned course. The reasons why planners seek participation are thus purely of a practical kind, and they have made no secret of their real intentions. In the context of a pioneering World Bank participatory programme (PIDER) in Mexico, Michael M Cernea recently noted that 'Participation of beneficiaries was the only avenue to pursue — not for just political or ideological reasons, but primarily for more efficiency and for reasons of an economic and technical nature.'[17]

What specific advantages do planners see in the participatory approach to development? First, many development projects will just not get off the ground if people do not come forward. The canal irrigation system is one such example.[18] If farmers do not cooperate among themselves, and with the project staff, there is no way to make irrigation schemes functional. Again, plans to increase agricultural production will not be effective if farmers are unwilling to use new agricultural technology and other inputs which the government extension agencies propagate. How critical participation is to agricultural production will be clear from the following observation, 'In many South-East Asian countries, an increase of 1 million tons in rice production requires the active participation of about

2 million farming families. Hence, attention to their problems is vital for success in increasing production.'[19]

Second, participation at the planning stage provides planners with information which is otherwise hard to come by. People in rural areas may be illiterate and ill-equipped to draw up blueprints for development, but they surely know (and often far more than the outside experts) what their real needs are, and also what should be done to meet those needs.[20] Often farmers'perspective 'sees' aspects of the situation which experts from outside are apt to overlook. However, there is a tendency to treat their knowledge of local things as of no avail. 'Those with formal education and training believe that their knowledge and skills are superior and that uneducated and untrained people must, by definition, be ignorant and unskilled.'[21]

Third, people accept change more willingly if they are involved in programmes designed to produce change in their lifestyle. A World Bank paper highlights this point, 'Community participation in the selection, design, construction and implementation of rural development programmes has often been the first step in the acceptance of change leading to the adoption of new techniques of production.'[22] Promoted without a proper understanding of socio-cultural aspects of rural life, many projects in the past have produced results just the opposite of what was intended.[23]

> . It is not uncommon that facilities and services are created and offered to the people, who then fail to use them satisfactorily. Many drinking water supply schemes have been set up, but the women, the traditional water-carriers, do not use the costly pumps installed by the programme agency. Rural housing is often built which people refuse to live in.... This happens when decision making processes exclude the participation of those affected....[24]

Participative decision-making produces better 'fit' between what people want and what the development agencies offer, and is thus more effective in accomplishing the project goals.

Fourth, studies have brought forth data which clearly suggest that participation reduces cost by mobilising unused labour and other local resources. Sylviane Fresson has documented the experience of a participatory scheme in small irrigation from Senegal.[25] This contradicts the opinion which regards development schemes based on participation of the local people as uneconomic, although politically necessary, and at best only marginal in their impact on development. A major contribution of this study lies in demonstrating that participation resulted in lower capital cost outlays than in usual irrigation schemes and succeeded in achieving both larger and more equitably distributed increases in agricultural incomes for people in the Matam region of Senegal. Cost considerations thus further contribute to the acceptability of participation.

Fifth, the involvement of people is known to have led to timely completion of many projects. Once people accept the project as their own and willingly come forward to implement it, they naturally become concerned to see that their labour starts bearing fruit as early as possible.[26]

Sixth, a related advantage is that once the project is ready, people willingly come forward to ensure that it operates efficiently and delivers the intended services. On the other hand, projects which are set up by external agencies without involving local participation do not enthuse the people.[27] Regardless of their technical soundness, such projects are looked on as mere intrusions from outside. As there is no commitment of the local population, problems quickly arise even about their normal maintenance and operation.

Seventh, the monitoring job which requires presence on the spot can be performed in a more effective manner by involving the local people. In fact, a view which is increasingly gaining ground is that the best monitoring system is one in which beneficiaries do some checking themselves. Since nobody can be more interested than the concerned people in seeing that projects are executed on time, use quality components,etc., their involvement is easily the most efficient way to curb the waste.[28]

Lastly, people learn how to promote their development by actually participating in the processes of planning, implementation, monitoring and evaluation. Thus participation is an educative process. It contributes to human resource development. Participation instils in the people a new confidence in their ability to mould their present as well as future through self-help efforts. One observer recently noted: 'The main justifying function of participation is development of man's essential powers — inducing human dignity and respect, and making men responsible for developing their powers of deliberate action.'[29] It is important that people develop a spirit of self-reliance.

External agencies can aid the development process only up to a point. Eventually it is the people themselves who have to shoulder responsibility for their development. The process must become part of the community ethos. Such gains cannot be measured in purely mathematical terms, but for this reason the advantages from participation cannot be dismissed as negligible. The intangible advantages are quite substantial.

Summing up, Rogers *et al.* list the following as among the specific benefits which accrue from involving people in their development.[30]

1. Villagers and the urban poor can be sources of useful ideas, such as those from indigenous technical knowledge.
2. They can help tailor technical ideas imported from the outside, so that these innovations are more workable under local conditions.
3. The users can act as experimenters and educators by testing new technologies or organisational arrangements.
4. They can also participate in decisions as to what development activities are conducted, so that their needs are more closely reflected in development programmes and commitment to implementation is reinforced.

Micheal M Cernea quotes the following to support his conclusion that the total development impact of enormous investments can simply be lost if there is no sufficient farmer participation:

PIDER experience shows that, without active participation of beneficiaries, projects in the communities do not achieve planned objectives and targets and, in the best of cases, operate poorly. In addition to being a waste of available resources, such poor results cause the communities to become discouraged and to lose interest and confidence in the efforts of government agencies to benefit them. Community passivity also compromises the objectives of PIDER: if beneficiaries are not involved in projects, the programme will do no more than build works and will make no contribution to promoting the self-sustaining development required to ensure that community members attain a more decent standard of living.[31]

Participation: What it is and What it is not

Not everybody is agreed on what participation means. The fact is that participation has come to mean different things to different people. A Philippine study identifies six modes of participation:

> The first mode involved only the educated and moneyed people in the community without the participation of the 'grassroots' or the beneficiaries. The second mode is one in which the people or beneficiaries are asked to legitimise or ratify projects identified as formulated by the government. In the third mode of partici-pation, the people are consulted about the project but they do not actually participate in the planning and management of pro-ject. In the fourth mode, the people are consulted from the very start and they actively participate in the planning and manage-ment of projects. In the fifth mode, the people or the beneficiaries are represented in the highest policy making body of the agency. Finally, in the sixth mode, the representatives of the people control the highest policy making body of the agency.[32]

Political aspects are often considered basic to participation. How-ever, participation is a much wider concept. Politically, the elec-tions held from time to time provide a mechanism to exercise con-trol over institutions and resources, but such controls may prove to be very elusive. Unless there are real opportunities for people to have a say in planning and implementation of their development, the adult franchise alone may mean nothing at all.[33] The real pur-pose of participation is to develop human capabilities for develop-ment decision-making and action. Participation means a kind of local autonomy in which people discover the possibilities of exercis-ing choice and, thereby, becoming capable of managing their own development.

Planners and people have their own reasons to regard participa-tion desirable. Participation is sought by planners chiefly for the untapped human resources it releases to help the development pro-cess along. For the people, participation is a means to gain easier access to public services and a greater degree of control over the delivery mechanisms. Sometimes the way planners and the people perceive participation differently can lead to situations that cannot be termed participatory. In most Third World countries, it is the elites who tend to acquire command of the development apparatus. On the other hand, in this kind of state-led development the common man increasingly finds himself caught up powerless to do anything concerning his own welfare. 'The participation of the masses in development is somewhat akin to the participation of the bullocks in ploughing done by the farmer. There is never any doubt as to whose design and decision is involved in this work.'[34] So unequal can become the relationship between planners and the poor, eliminating all chances of a real participatory experience.

Many situations which are taken for granted as constituting participation are, in fact, not so. Discussing farmer involvement in the context of irrigation projects, Lowdermilk and Lattimore define farmer involvement as 'having farmers participate in decision-making when planning, implementing and evaluating projects and programmes to improve the productivity and effectiveness of irrigation projects,' and have indicated several ways farmers can be involved in the improvement of irrigation projects:[35]

In identifying major problems.
In developing and testing solutions.
In planning activities for implementation of improvements.
Committing time, labour, cash and personal resources while implementing a project.
By leading the rehabilitation of farm systems, i.e., settling disputes, organising community labour, supervision of participation in construction.
By being responsible for the operation and maintenance of improved systems.

Further, comparing involvement with non-involvement, they spell out the following situations as not constituting farmer involvement:

Manipulating farmers for political purposes.
Involving only the elite farmers.
Using farmers to make a short-term project look good.
Using farmers by issuing orders or telling them what to do.
Using tricks to gain farmers' cooperation.
Using farmers to please outside agencies.
Arranging to give the impression that farmers are involved when

in reality they are not involved directly.
Using farmers to benefit projects that do not benefit the farmer.

Suggesting that participative policies cannot be simply 'added' to present policies, but must be part of a radically different overall approach, Emrich clarifies the meaning of participation through his six axioms. The axioms of participation are:

First, participation must begin at the very lowest level. There must be real opportunities for participative decision-making for the poorest, and those decisions must relate to the aspirations of the poor more than to the wispy musings of those who will not identify with them. Second, participation must take place at all stages of the development process, from the earliest pre-planning exercises, to the development of plans, the design of implementing mechanisms, and the actual implementation. Third, it must be recognised that a solitary vote is not participation. If people do not participate as members of relatively powerful groups which serve their interests, then they participate only for the benefit of their masters. Fourth, participation must have substance and usually political clubs and cooperatives do not have substance. 'Participative processes' must deal with the allocation and control of goods and services related to the production process. Fifth, participation must somehow deal with existing loyalties. If the result is merely to strengthen existing inter-class groupings it will just strengthen existing leadership. Sixth, it must be accepted that the development of effective participation will cause conflict in some form.[36]

Participation, as defined in a UNESCO document, is 'collective sustained activity for the purpose of achieving some common objectives, especially a more equitable distribution of the benefits of development.'[37] Although participation is defined in different ways, the dominant view is to regard it as a strategy to improve the development process. There seems to be general consensus that participation helps successful completion of projects, and that the impact of such development on people should be beneficial.

Two more points need to be stressed. First, discussion on participation largely centres round its uses in promoting rural development. This is understandable as a majority of people in Third World countries is still rural, and their development which was neglected all these years has now emerged as a matter of top priority. However, participatory processes are relevant to all sectors of development. Second, discussion on participation is mostly focused on participation at the local level. Actually it is here that participation can take place in the most direct manner possible. This is the level closest to people in their own little communities. However, participation can as well take place at higher levels — the district, the state and the centre.

It is important to understand the true meaning of participation, since failure to do so can lead to distortions in the processes and the end-products of development. This danger is real as participation is now emerging as a development idea acquiesced in by all, everywhere. '...participation is often endorsed unambiguously on normative grounds even if the empirical basis is not clear. A real danger is that with growing faddishness and a lot of lip service, participation could become drained of substance and its relevance to development programs disputable.'[38] Another cautionary note is that 'While participation can take the form of widespread rural mobilization to support and implement government policy, it can also serve as an effective tool for government control of the rural population.'[39] Used without properly understanding all the implications, participation can work both ways. It can well turn out to be the proverbial double-edged sword.

Emerging Participatory Organisations

Organisations that seek involvement of the poor from rural areas in programmes designed to further their development have now sprung up in many Third World countries.[40] Their forms range from cooperatives to water users' associations to women's organisations. Functions which these organisations perform can change the direction as well as the pace of development. Wanasinghe has identified five functions for such organisations: (*a*) identification of development goals, (*b*) agitation for the achievement of identified goals, (*c*) formulation of action programmes, (*d*) mobilisation of resources, and (*e*) organisation for the implementation of the action performance.[41] Uphoff and Easman have also identified six functions for local organisations: (*a*) planning and goal setting, (*b*) resource mobilisation, (*c*) provision of services, (*d*) integration of services, (*e*) control of administration, and (*f*) making claims.[42] In practice, the role which participatory organisations play depends on how participatory they really are.

Broadly speaking, rural organisations are of two kinds. One kind is that which the government generally sets up to elicit participation of the people in its development programmes. Panchayati Raj institutions in India fall in this category.[43] Such governmental organisations are sometimes referred to as standard rural organisations.

The other kind of organisation arises primarily from the initiative of the people themselves. Mutual aid societies, workers' associations, etc., are organisations that fall in this broad category. Such rural organisations are commonly referred to as non-governmental organisations (NGO). In order to distinguish these organisations from standard rural organisations, they are often referred to as participatory rural organisations. Another common name for them is voluntary organisations. Table 1 lists organisations of both the standard and the participatory kind which commonly exist in rural areas of Third World countries.

TABLE 1   *Standard and Participatory Rural Organisations*

Standard Organisations	Participatory Organisations
1. Cooperatives	1. Special organisations of rural disadvantaged groups, such as tenants' associations and organisations of agricultural labourers and landless workers
2. Village development committees	
3. Government sponsored farmers' organisations	
4. Trade unions	
5. Women's organisations	2. Village-based ad hoc organisations formed for a specific and immediate local need
6. Youth clubs	
7. Political party branches	
8. Development committees in new settlements	3. Village welfare associations
	4. Village funeral societies
9. Other voluntary organisations represented by the government	5. Kinship associations
	6. Caste associations
	7. Ethnic associations
	8. Irrigation associations
	9. Mutual aid work groups
	10. Rotating credit associations
	11. Religious associations

Source: Adapted from G Shabbir Cheema. 1983. The Role of Voluntary Organisations. *In* G Shabbir Cheema and Dennis A Rondinelli (eds.). 1983. *Decentralization and Development.* Beverly Hills: Sage. P. 210.

Based on studies of rural organisations in Asia, the Near East and Africa, a Food and Agriculture Organisation (FAO) report classifies rural organisations into two categories, namely, standard and participatory and describes characteristics of these organisations.[44]

STANDARD ORGANISATIONS

1. They are funded and sponsored by an outside, mostly government agency, with a top-bottom approach to development for the people, rather than a bottom-up approach. The idea is that benefits will trickle-down from above.
2. They are more formal and official.
3. Their set-up is often inspired by alien concepts, principles and policies frequently imported from abroad.
4. They are mostly elite-oriented and/or dominated with the result that the elite benefit more than others.

PARTICIPATORY ORGANISATIONS

1. They are started by the people themselves and not by a government or other outside agency.
2. They are more informal and unofficial.
3. They are more flexible in their objectives and in set-up.
4. Their leaders and their members are mainly the poor who reach decisions in face-to-face relationships (the term group or grouping often is more appropriate than the term organisation).
5. Their activities are related to the day-to-day situation and needs of the rural poor. The latter, understandably, are more attracted to join and participate actively in these groups than the official ones. ✔

Admittedly, no classificatory scheme can hope to cover fully the various types of rural organisations that have come into being in diverse settings. Classification of rural organisations into standard and participatory which the FAO study has suggested is a good attempt indeed. Cheema believes that with some modifications, this categorisation gets closest to the reality.[45]

Government-supported organisations easily dominate the rural scene. Their dominance is not due to numbers alone. On the other hand, the non-governmental organisations are not only few in number, but have also not grown to their full stature yet.[46] By themselves the people in villages are unable to form and manage organisations of their own. Resources and skills required for the job are scarce.[47] Although the poor are everywhere exhorted to organise, the rise of their organisations is often looked on with suspicion by most governments in Third World countries.

However, studies have demonstrated that people prefer to join organisations launched by their own groups rather than those which are set up by the government. The popularity of participatory organisations is explainable by the fact that these are better placed to serve the poor. Their area of operation is usually limited to a village, or a cluster of villages. This helps them to understand better the needs of the rural population. They are not bound by cumbersome rules and procedures. They are able to monitor progress of projects right on the spot. Further, their proximity to the people helps them secure their involvement in development more easily. These advantages more than offset the lack of resources and other limitations. A study in Philippines conducted for the FAO clearly highlights why people prefer to join community organisation (CO) style rural organisations and not the standard type rural organisations.[48] Table 2 summarises the findings of this study.

Many governments in the Third World have attempted to introduce new organisational structures at the grassroots level in the expectation that these will stimulate participation of the people in local developmental activities.[49] Realisation that the process of decentralisation is fundamental for securing involvement of the people has led them in this direction.[50]

In the 1950s the Panchayati Raj in India was established with very similar objectives: to involve the people in decisions about government initiated programmes, to facilitate the implementation of development projects, and to inculcate democratic values among the people.[51] The establishment of Panchayati Raj bodies at local levels followed devolution of decision-making authority, transfer of funds, personnel and other resources to local levels from higher levels in government, primarily from the State government.[52] In most cases, the Panchayati Raj institutions could not function in the manner envisaged, and by the late 1960s the original idea lost many of its adherents.[53] The reasons for decline are related to the fact that the local levels lacked expertise which was needed to cope with the growing complexities of development.[54] To carry forward the new development activities, several other official agencies have been inducted, some of which are area-based and others focused on disadvantaged groups.[55]

TABLE 2 *A Comparison of Reasons Why the Rural Poor Join CO Style Rural Organisations and Do Not Join Standard Rural Organisations*

Reasons Why Poor Join CO Style Organisations	Reasons Why Poor Do Not Join Standard Rural Organisations
1. Members themselves make the major decisions and carry them out. Incentives to join are high when participation is real	1. Elite leaders make most of the decisions and the members carry them out. Little incentive for participation
2. Members have a personal stake in the outcome of an activity because of involvement at all stages	2. As members are not involved much, their stake in the final outcome is limited
3. Leaders and members are from similar background. Commonality of interests enhances group solidarity	3. Leaders are from higher socio-economic background than the members. Their interests cannot be the same. If the clash of interests does not lead to open hostilities, it is because the poor are not prepared for a show down
4. Activities are informal. Election of leaders takes place later after they have proved their worth	4. Formal character requires that election be held first. When leaders do not perform well, they lose popular support
5. Leaders and members pool their efforts to achieve objectives they all consider are worth pursuing	5. There is no such involvement. Leaders and members are asked to respond to projects designed elsewhere
6. Mass action gives people the confidence, and enhances their dignity and self-respect	6. Being passive recipients of institutions, members rarely gain the experience of meaningful participation
7. Both leadership and membership are sought to be developed through training. All people know what the issues confronting them are, and leaders remain accountable	7. Outside agencies concentrate on training the leadership alone. Members feel alienated when leaders fail to communicate newly learnt skills to the people
8. Participation is broad based — old and young, men and women, big or small farmers all join. They respond to all concerns that matter to them	8. Categories of participants are specified, such as women with young children in nutrition programme. Participation is fragmented
9. From modest beginning as an informal group, the organisation	9. Members enter a full-blown organisation even before they

Reasons Why Poor Join CO Style Organisations	Reasons Why Poor Do Not Join Standard Rural Organisations
through experience matures into an organisation ready to face more challenging tasks	understand what it is. Not knowing what to do, they feel lost and only participate passively, if not drop out
10. Through various activities the organisation gives evidence of attempting to shift the local power structure to a more egalitarian one. This presents a vision for which the peasant is willing to follow an alternative mode of development	10. There is no attempt to change the local power structure. The vertical hierarchy of patron-client dependency offers to the poor the best alternative to survive or improve his life.

Source: Adapted from Mary Hollnsteiner *et al.* 1978. As quoted in Bernard van Hech. 1979. pp. 35-37.

However, the idea of decentralisation has not been abandoned.[56] The present emphasis on district planning and block-level planning is essentially an effort to decentralise the planning process.[57] There is a growing awareness that capability to envisage local level plans needs to be built up as a first step.[58] It is hoped that block-level planning will lead to establishment of appropriate organisations of the poor to protect them from exploitation and secure their active involvement in planning decisions.[59]

Experiences with the Participatory Programmes in Action

Even when participation has gained wide recognition as a basic human right, and its practical value in promoting development well established, the actual cases of participation do not add up to very much. On the basis of her African experience, Uma Lele concludes: 'Even where development of local participation is an important objective of rural development and where political education in mass participation is a key element of the development strategy, as in Tanzania, programmes have not developed genuine participation and responsibility among the rural people.'[60] Equally pessimistic is the conclusion of some other observers of development scene in the Third World.

A survey of the development scene, especially in the Third World countries, however, points to a disturbing tendency on the part of the national governments to push the people in the background. They are no more the subjects of development; they have become objects of development and in many cases even resources for development.

In country after country, popular institutions have gone into oblivion. Governments have extended their bureaucratic tentacles down to the village level. It is the official agencies which now initiate and carry out development on behalf of the people. The people themselves have become recipients of development as if development is something outside their realm of experience. Of course, there are rays of hope here and there, but the general scene is that of retrogression and despair.[61]

Participatory approaches are new to development practitioners, hence they lack experience in this area. Partly due to this reason, participatory programmes do not seem to be proceeding as well as they should. Often participatory schemes are launched without sufficient prior preparation.[62] In a hurry to produce quick results, the tasks of anticipating problems in the field and making provisions for dealing with unexpected situations are simply side-tracked.

Those concerned with the making of development plans tend to forget that participation cannot be achieved by plans formulated in isolation in central offices away from the people concerned. As one observer noted, the development agencies now

> Regularly incorporate its rhetoric in their development project plans — the reality seldom resembles the rhetoric. A growing body of evidence suggests that one explanation for the gap between rhetoric and reality can be found in the operating structures of organizations responsible for the implementation of development projects. Participation requires more than planning mandates and/or good will. It requires basic new skills and a reorientation of operating structures which plans alone cannot achieve.[63]

Elaborating this point on the basis of his own involvement in designing a participatory approach in Mexico, Jorge Echenique rightly observed:

> There is a tendency for rural development programs... to

emphasize farmer participation, organisation, and self-management.... But these goals are never actually defined or explained in detail.... As a result, this approach often goes no further than the pronouncement stage, and is not reflected or put into practice during the course of the program. The official agencies, whose inertia is evident, mostly act along their old hidebound traditional lines, defining what is to be done, how it is to be done, and who is to benefit, without having any specific knowledge of the real social and cultural context in which they are operating. Limited to a superficial view of the natural environment and resources, they entertain the native conviction that the aspirations and needs of the rural population match their own institutional priorities, and continue to dwell in the blissful certainty that the peasants know nothing of technology, projects, and serious things of that kind.[64]

However, many new participatory programmes are currently under way. This is a hopeful trend. Full accounts of projects from fields as diverse as irrigation systems, eco-system development, social forestry, water distribution, farm technology are now available.[65] Participation of women is emerging as a separate field of action.[66]

A SOCIOLOGICALLY DESIGNED WORLD BANK PARTICIPATORY PROGRAMME IN MEXICO

One large-scale programme designed to involve the participation of beneficiaries in their development is the World Bank-assisted rural development programme in Mexico called PIDER (PIDER is an acronym in Spanish for Integrated Programmes of Rural Development). This merits some discussion here for a novel sociological approach it has followed. The history and experiences involved in building up the rural development programme have been outlined in a paper which the World Bank has recently published.[67]

The PIDER programme was established in 1973 to transfer substantial resources for the implementation of small-scale, local projects in poor rural areas of Mexico. In about 10 years, this programme spent some US $ 2 billion to benefit 139 PIDER microregions, including over 9,000 communities with a population of about 12 million.

One distinguishing feature of PIDER is that its enormous resources are not being invested in a handful of large, visible and costly projects, but in numerous small projects, tailored to the specific needs of small villages and of sub-groups living in them. Projects for which investments have been made include small-scale irrigation schemes, soil conservation projects, fruit and tree plantations, rural roads, fishponds, livestock units, rural health centres, schools, potable water systems, village electrification, etc.

In the beginning very little was known about planning investments for communities with the active participation of the local population. However, these new approaches were preferred to the older ones, since very early it became obvious that traditional, top-down bureaucratic planning methods had some serious shortcomings, and that conventional planners lacking requisite local knowledge could not be expected to do justice to the job. Participation was accepted as PIDER's aim not for any higher, philosophical considerations but solely for reasons of efficient project implementation.

A methodology of participatory planning was worked out methodically. The approach adopted for the purpose was sociological in the sense that it was based on a comprehensive, step-by-step analysis of all the relevant social factors. The approach involved a sequence of designing, testing, learning, and revising the participatory procedures.

The farmer participation was seen as of critical importance in all the stages of planning, execution, supervision, etc., but particular stress was laid on ensuring participation in the initial stage involving programming of investments. Components of the programming work included: (*a*) establishing the priorities, (*b*) identifying the project beneficiaries, location and technology, and (*c*) determining the possible community contributions in cash or kind.

Social research (by a group of professionals from social anthropology, sociology, economics, and agronomy) which developed the methodology for participation was based on the premise that the farmers' perspective is a critical input for successful development planning and implementation. Expert knowledge is indispensable to the development process, but it was recognised that development cannot be planned exclusively on the basis of opinions of or studies by experts from outside. The officials do not necessarily have a better understanding of problems faced by the farmer. Participation helps peasants develop a definition of their interests and wants, without which they cannot be expected to act.

Social scientists who developed the participatory methodology were well aware that understanding the sociology of the community concerned was important, but was not enough. They did not regard techno-economic factors and financial feasibility considerations as of no consequence. On the contrary, it was accepted that sociological knowledge was complementary to, and not a substitute for, technical and other expertise. The linkage between the sociological and technical aspects of planning was consistently emphasised in the sociological participatory methodology.

PIDER experience not only validates soundness of the sociological approach in planning, implementation and monitoring of participatory development projects, specially programming of investments, but also highlights an aspect of this approach which is of great significance. The sociological approach developed for Mexico has transfer potential to other places, wherever participatory methodology is to be practised.

Constraints on Participation

Obstacles to participation abound; people encounter problems at every step all the way.[68] However, it is still not uncommon to blame the poor for their failure to participate in government-sponsored development activities. Those who do so probably are not aware of obstacles the poor face in efforts for their development. Not all the obstacles stem from reluctance of the poor.

Studies of the factors that help or hinder participation have revealed how strong the anti-participatory forces can be, compared to the participatory ones.[69] In her study on participation, Frances F Korten discovered several powerful obstacles to participation by the poor.[70] She has classified these into three broad categories, (a) obstacles within the agency, (b) obstacles within the community, and (c) obstacles within the society.

There are some constraints which arise locally. These constraints have to do mainly with the people themselves, their lifestyle and the communities they live in. These factors are primarily socio-cultural, and can be called internal constraints. There are others which are external to the individual and the community he lives in. These constraints have to do mainly with the administrators, their values and attitudes, and the way they are organised for development work in villages. Being essentially bureaucratic, these factors can be called external constraints.

SOCIO-CULTURAL CONSTRAINTS (INTERNAL)

Until recently, it was widely assumed that the deeply ingrained attitudes of fatalism among village people hinder the participatory process. It was assumed that peasants were happy with the things around them, and that they had no aspirations to change their ways.[71] Now substantial evidence from anthropological and other studies has come in which makes such assumptions completely untenable.[72]

Admittedly, participation still does not fascinate many rural poor.[73] However, this lack of interest in their own development has nothing to do with the attitudes of fatalism, the innate conservatism and other such traits which have been attributed to them for too long. As a matter of fact, it is their past experience with governmental agencies which holds them back. Participation appears quite irrelevant to the poor in their circumstances. Rather they prefer to seek help from their families, landlords, money-lenders, shop-keepers, and from anyone who may be a friend in need.[74]

A significant factor restricting participation by the poor is their low level of awareness. Governmental assistance seems irrelevant because many people are simply not aware of public services which exist for them right in their own village. The elite groups tend to monopolise all contacts with the outside agents. Often the poorer groups see no point in competing with the more affluent for services and benefits which the contacts bring. Explaining why the poor regard participation as of no particular concern to them, Huntington and Nelson have outlined three basic reasons for this situation:

There are several reasons for this low efficacy. First, the poor lack resources for effective participation — adequate information, appropriate contacts, money, and often time. Second, in low-income strata, people are often divided by race, tribe, religion or language; even where the cleavages are not obvious, distinctions may be drawn on the basis of differences in sect, income, status, or place of origin that outsiders can barely perceive. More privileged groups may draw similar distinctions, but they are often better able to cooperate across such lines when joint economic or political interests are at stake. Third, the poor tend to expect requests or pressures on their part, whether individual or collective, to be ignored or refused by the authorities and these expectations are often justified. Worse, their attempts may provoke governmental repression or prompt reprisals from the private interests threatened by the self-assertion of the poor. Those on the margin of subsistence are particularly vulnerable to threats from employers, landlords, or creditors.[75]

If participation is to be meaningful, there should be participatory local organisations of the poor. By linking with development agencies of the government at the village level, the local organisations can provide to the members a forum to participate in the designing and implementation of development programmes.[76] However, the number of villages without local organisations is much larger than the number of villages with local organisations. Even where organisations of the poor have been in existence for some time, they do not seem to be functioning very well in projecting their demands and otherwise helping their cause.[77] The poor simply lack necessary skills in organising and managing their affairs collectively. Electing capable leaders, calling meetings, making decisions, keeping records, raising subscriptions, and handling funds are some of the tasks that require for their performance a certain degree of managerial ability. Generally the poor in villages lack these skills and thus are not in a position to establish organisations of their own to promote development. This factor severely limits the emergence of participatory processes.[78]

BUREAUCRATIC CONSTRAINTS (EXTERNAL)

A major external constraint on participation is the bureaucracy itself. Constraints are inherent in the very body politic and routines of the bureaucratic machinery.[79] Most government-administered development agencies came into existence long before participation became part of the current development philosophy. They were designed with a centralised, service-delivery approach in view where flexibility and responsiveness to needs in the field have no place. Therefore, these programme agencies lack development orientation.[80] Participation and such innovative ideas are in fact an anthema to it. Observers of bureaucratic behaviour all agree that 'finding ways of inculcating the spirit of experimentation and creativity into hierarchical and control-oriented bureaucracies has eluded most administrative reformers.'[81]

Bureaucrats seriously believe that they alone have answers to all problems faced by the poor and that they are the only ones who have a right to this knowledge. In their scheme of things, the only role people can and should play is to act as mere recipients of the delivery system. 'Bureaucratic processes in large organizations have instilled in most government employees a respect for technocratic knowledge and expertise and a disdain for their clients' capabilities in conceptualizing, designing and implementing programs.'[82] However, to be effective the participatory approach requires that there be a sense of partnership between administrators and the people. If this condition is not fulfilled, there will hardly be any scope for people to participate in the development process. The bureaucratic paternalism turns the rural poor into passive recipients of governmental services.

Disdain for capabilities of the poor is not the only reason why administrators discourage participation. As a matter of fact, they feel uncomfortable with working methods that involve consultation. Participatory methodology entails frequent visits to villages instead of working in the comfort of their offices in the capital. If this approach is followed, the job of activating the village community cannot be left to extension agents as was the case before. On the other hand, 'It is far easier for bureaucrats to decide what the people should want, relate that to government objectives and draw up plans accordingly, than to consult the millions who are supposed to benefit from those plans.'[83]

One fear that commonly grips the bureaucracies is that, if lower level officials are delegated more functions and responsibility, things are bound to go wrong. Decision-making authorities at the higher level invariably view the officials lower down the hierarchy as lacking in competence, and hence untrustworthy. Decentralisation is impossible to practise in such circumstances.[84]

Often communication between different hierarchical levels breaks down for very similar reasons. In order to show off their superior status, the higher level administrators begin to maintain more and more distance from the lower level officials in the field. As a result, they only end up denying to themselves feedback which can be critical to programme implementation. Confronted with aloofness on the part of their superiors, the staff in the field also begins to withdraw into its own shell, leaving the people to their own devices. It has been rightly observed: 'In an environment where project staff cannot meaningfully participate, it is highly unlikely that they will encourage participation on the part of those they are supposedly trying to help.'[85]

The highly centralised character of bureaucracies does not allow the field staff any discretion to act. Their inability to act when the local situation demands that certain things be done promptly discourages the people to come forth. Rather than act and as a result get into trouble, the field staff prefers to sit back, and await orders from above. Often it is safer not to act than to act. 'Just as the small farmer wishes to minimize risk, so does the bureaucrat.'[86]

Even as things presently stand, opportunities for promotion and other incentives, especially for the staff in the field, are virtually non-existent. Rather than concentrate on work in villages, many find it more rewarding to just keep their immediate superiors in good humour, pandering to the bureaucratic emphasis on meeting targets somehow or the other.[87]

Using money spent as the criterion to evaluate performance has led to shifts in favour of larger projects. Participation is not a requirement of such projects. Work is contracted to outside agencies, and this is justified on grounds of quality, savings in time as well as money.

In recent years, the government-run development agencies have rapidly proliferated. However, there is very little effective coordination in their working even when the goals they pursue are similar.[88] The result of their failure to harmonise operations at the field level means that the farmer must run from agency to agency. A simple thing like getting seed on credit involves visits to several agencies, not once but several times. Often the farmer must run around at a time when he is rather busy performing agricultural operations. Disheartened, there are many who simply give up the effort to get help from governmental agencies ostensibly established to involve them in development programmes.

Promoting Participation in Development

Occasional exhortations will not help produce participation. People must be empowered to take the necessary steps.[89] Simultaneously, bureaucracy needs to be reoriented as the government has a major responsibility for furthering development.[90]

The way to actualise participation is to first consider the nuts-and-bolts question in a thorough-going manner. Such a discussion is often restricted by the fact that enough is still not known about how participation actually occurs in different settings. The kind of questions which are relevant to development agencies and administrators were raised in a symposium on World Bank-assisted participation projects. These questions were summed up by Gloria Davis:

> The questions, then, are: How do we increase participation? What are the costs? ... What are the contextual factors which make success more or less probable? How do we address problems such as class stratification and different class interests within villages? How do we link village demands with vertically integrated implementing agencies with a divergence of budgets and policies? And how do we deal with the development objectives, ideologies, and vested interests of borrower Governments? These questions are not an argument against a participatory approach, but suggest that what is needed is not only the willingness to do participatory projects, but a tool kit of concepts and examples on how to proceed....[91]

The obstacles look formidable, but attempts to involve people in recent years have been fairly productive. Encouraged by these results, development agencies and experts are now trying to formulate guiding principles for participatory projects.[92]

EMPOWERING THE RURAL POOR

The people must be helped to help themselves. At the present stage of their development they certainly need considerable support. Without help from outside, they would not be in a position to benefit from development programmes specially designed for them. If they are not assisted properly, new programmes will lead to further dependency. The local capacity needs to be built up first.

If people have to be active partners in designing projects and later have to work closely with government agencies in implementation, monitoring and evaluation, they must make a resource commitment which could be in either cash or kind. This is considered desirable for several reasons:

> First, governments do not have the resources to support all worthwhile development initiatives. Requiring an initial resource commitment indicates that this is not going to be another government 'giveaway' program. Many activities would probably function better without the involvement of government at all. Second, the act of making a resource commitment will make the contributors more concerned for the success of the development initiative than they otherwise might be. Finally, such a commitment will provide a concrete indication of how interested the community members are in a new initiative. Findings from an earlier study demonstrated the positive correlation between such resource commitment and the overall project success.[93]

Even the attitudes of development personnel undergo some change when they discover that the people are making contributions. Cernea writes:

> In fact, the official requirement that local communities contribute a fraction of investment costs turns out to affect not only communities, but the technicians' behaviour as well: it makes the planners and engineers more concerned with consulting the peasants than before, with getting the peasants' assent and contribution, and with actually involving them in the works.[94]

If participation is to be a self-sustained process, one that will not wither away once the development teams depart, the people have to be taught certain skills. Knowledge and information are crucial to make participation a continuing activity and to give the people an idea of what their rights and responsibilities are. Therefore, training can be extremely useful to the people in villages. Recently the following were identified as major skills which can help build up the local capacity for participation: (*a*) managerial skills; (*b*) internal organisational management skills; (*c*) economic resource management skills; (*d*) technical skills; and (*e*) political skills.[95] This list is only illustrative; it is not exhaustive.

Local organisations of the poor do not exist everywhere. Even where they do, they are not in a very good shape. This situation does not help the participatory processes. Very little is known about these organisations and their capability for interaction with official implementation agencies in rural areas.[96] There is a tendency to set up new organisations to promote development, and to dismiss the existing traditional organisations and networks as of no particular relevance to development work.[97] Experience indicates that indigenous organisations can prove to be far more dynamic in mobilising people to join hands with official agencies in the promotion of various development programmes.[98]

All these years, the farmer's behaviour has been seen as irrational, opposed to anything new coming from outside his immediate environment. The truth is that his reactions, including rejections of outside interventions, are completely sensible in the very adverse circumstances that surround him. If anything, there is a need to understand his viewpoint and things that interest him.[99] Often technology is sought to be introduced which is appropriate, not from his angle but, from the perspective of its promoters. An evaluation study by UNDP recently concluded that one major constraint

affecting achievement of project objectives is the transfer of technologies without local adaptation. These often show no advantage over local technologies. Even if there is an advantage, it is often nullified by lack of understanding or by resentment of a new idea 'parachuted' into an area without previous consultation with the users. There have also been attempts to alter local conditions to suit the new technology, instead of the reverse.[100]

Many mistakes can be easily avoided if attention is paid to understanding the lifestyle of the poor in villages. Unfortunately, planners do not seem to attach due importance to this knowledge. In the context of the PIDER project in Mexico for which a social methodology of participation was specially designed it was rightly observed:

While many technologies are available for the 'hardware' components of development projects, this is not the case for the institutional components and the socio-cultural parts of these projects, which in no way are less important for the project's ultimate success. Yet methodologies for software development are generally not available in a conceptualized and operationalized form; development agencies have not joined efforts with the social science communities for elaborating them.[101]

However, the importance of sociological and anthropological studies is now being readily accepted. A World Bank Task Force on Poverty recently noted:

> To support and selectively finance rural development activities that benefit poor people, the Bank should increase its understanding of patterns of social organization in project areas. This requires more reliance on local socio-anthropological expertise than is usually the case. Successes and failures in participatory activity with the rural poor should be reviewed and this learning incorporated in future projects.[102]

ADAPTING ADMINISTRATION TO PARTICIPATORY DEVELOPMENT

Working in the field on people-centred projects, administrators confront some very specific dilemmas:[103]

Access: Which groups or members of the public should be included?

Responsiveness: To whom should administrators be responsive, to the organised public or the unorganised and less visible public?

Professionalism: What is the best way to evaluate citizen preferences when they contradict professional training and judgment?

Effectiveness: What can an administrator do if organised publics either veto or dilute a project so that little is done?

Like administrators, the people also face certain dilemmas. They know that administrators may not always be responsive to their needs. People are quite certain that they can be easily bypassed by administrators whose accountability is not to them but to their agencies and their superiors. Therefore, the people look at the same problems differently:

Access: Assuming that bureaucrats are trying to build coalitions with supporters, what voice or access can non-supporters have? *Responsiveness*: Administrators often benefit from the participatory process. But what about those instances when this is not the case and opposition threatens them? How can the concept of loyal opposition be instilled? What recourse do the poor — the peasants — have, to be taken seriously?

Professionalism: Based on their professionalism, administrators may readily assume they know what is best for project beneficiaries and others in the community; this presupposition is particularly popular in the Third World, where there is often a great social distance between bureaucrats and the public. At the same time it is easy for the public to be intimidated by the expertise and training of administrators. The problem for citizens is, therefore, to develop an independent source of authority.

Effectiveness: The public may define effectiveness very differently than administrators; peasants for example, may have other goals they are seeking quite separate from those of the experts.

Thus administrators and the people do not view the participatory process alike. Differences in their perceptions are quite significant. One way to incorporate their divergent viewpoints is to view participation as a learning process, as mutual interaction. In the development community there is a growing consensus that 'creating effective participation is a gradual, evolutionary process in which both project staff and potential beneficiaries are willing to try various alternatives, discard them when they prove unworkable and try others.'[104]

The 'blueprint' approach, which assumes that solutions to problems are all known and that predetermined intervention techniques are certain to produce expected results in a given situation, is unlikely to be as successful as the 'process' approach. By contrast, the process approach assumes that there are many imponderables in life and, therefore, it is marked by constant openness to redesign and adaptation to changing situations. Studies of problems on the ground and an interactive style of problem solving are preferred to remote expertise.[105] Honadale *et al.* sum up the strength and potential of the process approach:[106]

It is rooted in dialogue with the rural population and thus is more responsive to local potential and needs than the more technically oriented blueprint.

It allows variation in bureaucratic structures and thus is more likely to adapt to political, social, economic, and physical changes that occur during implementation.

It is based on learning and capacity building and it is well fitted to the promotion of self-sustaining development dynamics.

It transfers 'ownership' of the programme to implementers and thus creates an environment supportive of innovative problem solving rather than routine application of predetermined solutions.

It avoids negative side effects by eliminating design components that are deemed inappropriate.

Adapting administration to make it effective in coping with the complexities of participatory development is a task that must be tackled at all levels of the government. Improvements will not come about by concentrating efforts only at the top. Reorientation is most needed at grassroots level where officials come in direct, face-to-face contact with the people. One reason for the overall poor administrative performance is that administrative reform is seen more relevant to operations at higher levels alone and, therefore, improvement efforts are mostly concentrated at the centre rather than at the periphery. On the basis of a study in South-East Asian countries, Milton Easman concluded:

> One of the main findings of this paper, however, is that governments have been concentrating too much on administrative improvement and reform at the ministerial and regional levels, often through elaborate planning and coordinating structures. Too little attention is being devoted to the local level where government staff and programmes actually reach or fail to reach their rural publics. The greatest weakness of rural development administration is in the underdevelopment of administrative capabilities and of local institutions on the ground. It is to the correction of these limitations and imbalances that the main efforts of governments and international donors should be directed.[107]

Experience suggests that concentrating improvement efforts only at the higher levels can prove counterproductive. In Liberia, considerable resources were expended on strengthening a marketing project management unit. However, the overall impact was not favourable. The staff in the newly equipped unit became even more reluctant to delegate marketing functions to the local units. Their excuse was that the local units were not capable enough to perform well, whereas the project management unit now was.[108]

The direction in which the administration must move to become more responsive is a subject that has lately evoked great interest.[109] No formula which can be applicable to all situations can possibly emerge. Yet it might be worthwhile to recapitulate here suggestions for improvement emanating from various studies.[110]

Decision-making powers must move from the centre to the periphery. Beneficiary participation is unlikely to go far in situations where field level officials themselves have no say in any matter. Coordination mechanisms must pursue the single aim of making public services easily accessible to the people. More objective criteria to evaluate performance of development personnel must be devised, so that the staff concentrate on their actual task of serving the poor. The field staff is accountable only to its superiors, and to no one else. There must be some accountability to the people as well whom alone it is supposed to serve. The field workers must get the feeling that they really are involved in a challenging task. More incentives are needed to motivate them for work in arduous conditions of rural areas.[111]

Above all, attitudes of the field staff should change. They must recognise that the new task cannot be handled with the old attitudes of the predevelopment era. The workers must view their role as responding to needs of the people rather than simply expecting the people to respond in a sheep-like manner to governmental initiatives.

The potential of training in equipping the field personnel for participatory projects has not been fully realised yet.[112] Most training programmes continue to emphasise technical aspects of the job. Skills for working with the people are usually not included in the curricula design. Emphasising the urgency of developing skills for participatory development, Norman Uphoff noted: 'Orienting the technical staff toward fruitful collaboration with rural communities is not easy, but it is absolutely necessary.'[113]

Even in the best of circumstances, the administration of programmes in which people are expected to play a significant role cannot be an easy task. The World Development Report 1983, focused on problems of management in development, noted:

> People-centred programmes are particularly hard to manage because of the degree of uncertainty. First, goals can be abstract ('community self-reliance', for example) and performance not quantifiable in terms of construction time and costs or profits and losses. Second, there is little knowledge of how to design suitable programmes, because they involve changing human behaviour patterns that vary among cultures and localities. Third, the success of a project depends on whether people want the services it offers; project managers therefore often have to create demand. The task of management is thus more one of experimenting and learning than of implementing known procedures....[114]

No wonder, the job of adapting administration to the requirements of a participatory development has defied many past attempts. At the same time, some of the successes achieved are quite remarkable. Successes have been reported from wide geographic areas for a variety of programmes.[115] One key lesson from the development experience, as the World Development Report 1980 notes, is that it takes a long time to build up effective institutions. Persistence counts here the most. Governments and the concerned international agencies should neither expect magical results, nor give up too easily.[116]

NOTES AND REFERENCES

1. Samuel P. Huntington and Joan M. Nelson. 1976. *No Easy Choice: Political Participation in Developing Countries*. Cambridge, Mass: Harvard University Press. P. 1.
2. Daniel Lerner. 1958. *The Passing of Traditional Society*. Glencoe, Ill: The Free Press. P. 50.
3. On Participation in Federal Republic of Germany, see Adolf Herkenrath, Citizen Participation in Administrative Action. *In* Hari Mohan Mathur and Helmut Palla (eds.). 1983. *Local Administration and Regional Development*. Berlin: German Foundation for International Development/Kuala Lumpur: Asian and Pacific Development Centre. Pp. 197-205.

4. Lucy Mair. 1962. *Primitive Government.* Harmondsworth: Penguin Books Ltd.

5. Poona Wignaraja. 1984. Towards a Theory and Practice of Rural Development. *Development: Seeds of Change,* 1984: 2-3-11, p. 7.

6. United Nations. 1975. *Popular Participation in Decision-Making for Development.* New York: UN Department for Economic and Social Affairs. Also see, Lothar A. Kotzsch. 1984. People's Participation as a Task of Planning (Nepal). *Development and Cooperation,* No. 3, May-June 1984, pp. 24-25.

7. William F. Wertheim and Mathias Stiefel. 1982. *Production, Equity and Participation in Rural China.* Geneva: UNRISD.

8. Peter Oakley and David Marsden. 1984. *Approaches to Participation in Rural Development* (A WEP Study). Geneva: International Labour Office. Also see, Paul Harrison. 1980. *The Third World Tomorrow.* Harmondsworth: Penguin Books Ltd.

9. Harsh Sethi. 1983. *Development Issues in South Asia: The State, Voluntary Agencies, and the Rural Poor.* Paper presented to the Second International FFHC/AD Consultation, Rome, 13-16 September 1983.

10. Michael M. Cernea (ed.). 1985. *Putting People First: Sociological Variables in Rural Development Projects.* New York: Oxford University Press.

11. Robert Chambers. 1983. *Rural Development: Putting the Last First.* London: Longman.

12. Guy Gran. 1983. *Development by People.* New York: Praeger. Also see, David C. Korten and Rudi Klauss (eds.). 1984. *People Centered Development: Contributions toward Theory and Planning Frameworks.* West Hartford: Kumarian Press.

13. The Cocoyoc Declaration is United Nations Document A/C2/292 of November 1974.

14. Everett M. Rogers, Nat J. Colletta and Joseph Mabindyo. 1980. Social and Cultural Influences on Human Development. *In* Peter T. Knight (ed.). 1980. *Implementing Programs of Human Development.* Washington D C: The World Bank (Staff Working Paper No. 403). P. 263.

15. E.R. Morss and others. 1976. *Strategies for Small Farmer Development.* Boulder, Colorado: Westview Press.

16. See the chapter People's Participation in Development. *In* IFAD. 1981. *Annual Report 1981.* Rome: International Fund for Agricultural Development. Pp. 27-32.

17. Michael M. Cernea. 1983. *A Social Methodology for Community Participation in Local Investments: The Experience of Mexico's PIDER Program.* Washington D C: The World Bank (Staff Working Paper No. 598). P. 4.

18. United Nations. 1976. *Rural Development, the Small Farmer and Institutional Reform.* Bangkok: UNESCAP. P. 75.

19. M. S. Swaminathan. 1983. *Agricultural Progress: Key to Third World Prosperity* (Third World Lecture 1983). London: Third World Foundation. P. 10.

20. David W. Brokensha, D.M. Warren and Oswald Werner (eds.). 1980. *Indigenous Systems of Knowledge and Development.* Lanham MD: University Press of America, Inc.

21. Robert Chambers. 1979. Editorial on Indigenous Knowledge. *IDS Bulletin,* 10: 1-3.

22. World Bank. 1975. *Rural Development: Sector Policy Paper.* Washington D C: The World Bank. P. 37.

23. David Pitt. 1976. *The Social Dynamics of Development.* Oxford: Pergamon Press.
24. Samuel Paul. 1983. *Strategic Management of Development Programmes.* Geneva: ILO. P. 95.
25. Sylviane Fresson. 1980. Public Participation on Village Level Irrigation Perimeters in the Matam Region of Senegal. *In* Duncan Miller (ed.). 1980. *Studies on Rural Development.* Vol. II. *Studies on Rural Water Supply Schemes.* Paris Development Centre of the OECD. Pp. 96-161.
26. A. H. Barclay. 1970. The Development Impact of Private Voluntary Organizations. *Development Digest,* 17(3), 105-24, July 1979.
27. J. Waddimba. 1979. *Some Participative Aspects of Programmes to Involve the Poor in Development.* Geneva: UNRISD.
28. Mathias Stiefel and Mathias Wessler. 1983. Monitoring, Evaluation, and Participation: Some Common Fallacies and New Orientations. *Dialogue About Participation,* 4 (33-38), 1983.
29. Mary R. Hollnsteiner. 1976. People Power: Community Participation in the Planning and Implementation of Human Settlements. *Philippines Studies,* Vol. 24, 1976, p. 8.
30. Everett M. Rogers, Nat J. Colletta and Joseph Mabindyo. 1980. P. 263.
31. Quoted in Michael M. Cernea. 1983. P. 85.
32. Mary R. Hollnsteiner. 1976.
33. George Kent. Community-Based Development Planning. *Third World Planning Review,* Vol. 3, No. 3, August 1981, pp. 313-26.
34. Kishore Saint. Development and People's Participation. *In* Walter Fernandes (ed.). 1980. *People's Participation in Development.* New Delhi: Indian Social Institute. Pp. 3-10; 4-5.
35. Max Lowdermilk and Dan Lattimore. 1981. *Farmer Involvement* (Planning Guide No. 2). Logan, UT: Utah State University. P. 3.
36. Keith R. Emrich. Participation: Cure or Whitewash? *In* Inayatullah (ed.). 1979. *Approaches to Rural Development: Some Asian Experiences.* Kuala Lumpur: APDAC/347-373. P. 360.
37. UNESCO. 1979. *Meeting of Experts on the Institutional Problems of Participation in the Strategies of Integrated Rural Development.* Lima, Peru, 4-8 September 1978. Paris: UNESCO, Division for the Study of Development. P. 15.
38. Norman T. Uphoff, John M. Cohen and Arthur A. Goldsmith. 1979. *Feasibility and Application of Rural Development Participation: A State-of-the Art Paper.* Ithaca, NY: Cornell University Press. P. 3.
39. David D. Gow and Jerry VanSant. 1981. *Beyond the Rhetoric of Rural Development Participation: How Can it Be Done?* Washington DC: Development Alternatives, Inc. P. 5.
40. Lenore Ralston, James Anderson and Elizabeth Colson. 1983. *Voluntary Efforts in Decentralized Management.* Berkeley: University of California, Institute of International Studies.
41. H. S. Wanasinghe. Role of Peasant Organizations in Rural Development. *In* Inayatullah (ed.). 1979. Pp. 320-21.
42. Norman T. Uphoff and Milton J. Easman. 1974. *Local Organizations for Development: Analysis of Asian Experience.* Ithaca, NY: Cornell University, Centre for International Studies. Pp. 16-17.

43. Iqbal Narain. Democratic Decentralization and Rural Leadership in India: The Rajasthan Experiment. *Asian Survey*, Vol. 4, No. 8, August 1964.
44. Bernard Van Heck. 1979. *Participation of the Poor in Rural Organizations.* Rome: FAO of the UN. Pp. 24-25.
45. G. Shabbir Cheema. 1983. The Role of Voluntary Organizations. *In* G. Shabbir Cheema and Dennis A. Rondinelli. 1983. *Decentralization and Development: Policy Implementation in Developing Countries.* Beverly Hills: Sage Publications. P. 209.
46. K. C. Alexender. 1980. Emergence of Peasant Organizations in South India. *Economic and Political Weekly*, 15(26), 28 June 1980, A 72-A 87.
47. Abdul Aziz. 1983. *The Rural Poor: Problems and Prospects.* New Delhi: Ashish Publishing House.
48. Mary Racelis Hollnsteiner, Bejamin Bagadion, Jr., Fernadez Ricardo, Cecilia Cano, Corazon Jaliano, Eduardı Tadem and Frances Vega. 1978. *Development From the Bottom-up: Mobilizing the Rural Poor for Self-Development.* Manila, 1978. (Country study carried out for WACRRD and ROAP, FAO Rome).
49. David K. Leonard and Dale Rogers Marshal (eds.). 1982. *Institutions of Rural Development for the Poor.* Berkeley: University of California, Institute of International Studies.
50. Alec McCallum. 1981. *Decentralization in Support of the Small Farmer.* Paper for Inter-regional Seminar on Decentralisation for Development. Khartoum, Sudan, 14-18 September 1981. Organised by the UN DTCD Division of Development Administration.
51. P. C. Mathur. 1982. Institutional Genesis of Panchayati Raj in Rajasthan. *In* Mohan Mukerji (ed.). 1982. *Administrative Innovations in Rajasthan.* New Delhi: Associated Publishing House. Pp. 1-21.
52. Henry Maddick. 1970. *Panchayati Raj: A Study of Rural Local Government in India.* London: Longman.
53. P. C. Mathur. 1977. Performance of Panchayati Raj Institutions in Rajasthan, 1959-1974: A Critical Survey. *Social Change*, September-December 1977, 16-30.
54. Government of India. 1978. *Report of the Committee on Panchayati Raj Institutions.* New Delhi: Ministry of Agriculture and Irrigation, Department of Rural Development.
55. Noorjahan Bava. 1984. *People's Participation in Development Administration in India.* New Delhi: Uppal Publishing House.
56. R. N. Haldipur. 1971. On Remodelling Panchayati Raj. *The Indian Journal of Public Administration*, Vol. XVII, No. 3, July-September 1971.
57. R. P. Misra and K. V. Sundaram. 1980. *Multi-Level Planning and Integrated Rural Development in India.* New Delhi: Heritage Publishers.
58. United Nations. 1980. *The Practice of Local Level Planning.* Bangkok: UN Economic and Social Commission for Asia and the Pacific.
59. Government of India. 1979. *Report of the Working Group on Block-Level Planning.* New Delhi: Planning Commission.
60. Uma Lele. 1975. *The Design of Rural Development: Lessons from Africa.* Baltimore: The Johns Hopkins University Press. P. 162.
61. R. P. Misra and G. Shabbir Cheema. 1983. Group Action and Popular Participation. *In* R. P. Misra (ed.). 1983. *Local Level Planning and Development.* New Delhi: Sterling Publishers. P. 231.

62. Coralie Bryant and Louise G. White. 1980. *Managing Rural Development: Peasant Participation in Rural Development.* West Hartford, Connecticut: Kumarian Press.
63. Felipe B. Alfonso. 1983. Assisting Farmer Controlled Development of Communal Irrigation Systems. *In* David C. Korten and Felipe B. Alfonso (eds.). 1983. *Bureaucracy and the Poor: Closing the Gap.* West Hartford, Connecticut: Kumarian Press. P. 44.
64. Jorge Echenique. 1979. *Notes on Peasant Participation in Rural Development Planning.* Paper prepared for the Sociological Workshop on Participation, 8 August 1979. Washington DC: The World Bank. (mimeo). P. 1. Quoted here from Michael M. Cernea. 1983.
65. See, N.G.R. De Silva 1981. Farmer Participation in Water Management: The Minipe Project in Sri Lanka. *Rural Development Participation Review*, 3(1), Fall 1981, 16-19; T.K. Jayaraman. 1980. People's Participation in the Implementation of Watershed Management Project: An Empirical Study from Gujarat. *The Indian Journal of Public Administration*, 26(4), October-December 1980, 1009-16; Kanwar Prakash Chand and Ranveer Singh. 1983. People's Participation and Social Forestry: A Case Study of Himachal Pradesh. *Indian Journal of Agricultural Economics*, Vol. XXXIII, No. 3, July-September 1983, pp. 317-22; M. L. Santhanam. 1984. Community Participation: A Case Study. *Social Change*, Vol. 14, No. 2, June 1984, pp. 48-52; M. L. Dewan and Sudhirender Sharma. 1985. *People's Participation in Himalayan Eco-system Development.* New Delhi: Centre for Policy Research.
66. UNDP. 1980. *Rural Women's Participation in Development* (Evaluation Study No. 3). New York: United Nations Development Programme.
67 This section draws on Michael M. Cernea. 1983. *A Social Methodology for Community Participation in Local Investments: The Experience of Mexico's PIDER Program.* Washington DC: The World Bank (Staff Working Paper No. 598).
68. Guy Gran. 1979. Six Generic Difficulties for Participation in Development. *In* USAID. 1979. *Some Functional Constraints to Enhancing Participation in Project Design and Implementation.* Washington DC: USAID.
69. Ma Concepcion P. Alfiler. 1983. Factors that Promote or Deter Popular Participation in Development: The Philippine Experience. *Philippine Journal of Public Administration*, Vol. XXII, No. 1, January 1983, pp. 23-41.
70. Frances F. Korten. 1983. Community Participation: A Management Perspective on Obstacles and Options. *In* David C. Korten and Felipe B. Alfonso (eds.). 1983. Pp. 181-200.
71. Everett M. Rogers. 1966. Motivation, Values and Attitudes of Subsistence Farmers: Toward a Sub-culture of Peasantry. *In* Cliffton R. Wharton, Jr. (ed.). 1966. *Subsistence Agriculture and Economic Development.* Chicago: Aldine.
72. Hans-Dieter Evers (ed.). 1973. *Modernization in South-East Asia.* Singapore: Oxford University Press.
73. Carl Widstrand. 1976. Rural Participation in Planning. *In* David C. Pitt (ed.). 1976. *Development From Below: Anthropologists and Development Situations.* The Hague: Mouton.
74. Raymond Firth and B. S. Yamey (eds.). 1964. *Capital, Saving and Credit in Peasant Societies.* London: George Allen and Unwin Ltd.
75. Samuel P. Huntington and Joan M. Nelson. 1976. P. 118.

76. Koenread Verhagen. 1980. How to Promote People's Participation in Rural Development through Local Organizations. *Review of International Cooperation*, 73(1), 11-28.

77. George B. Verghese. 1981. Voluntary Agencies: How Useful? *Ideas and Action*, (142), 4-6.

78. G. Shabbir Cheema. 1981. Nongovernmental Organizations, the Rural Poor and Regional Development: An Asian Perspective. *In* R. P. Misra (ed.). 1981. *Humanizing Development*. Singapore: Maruzen Asia. Pp. 255-80.

79. George Honadle and Rudi Klauss (eds.). 1979. *International Development Administration*. New York: Praeger.

80. Merilee Grindle (ed.). 1980. *Politics and Policy Implementation in the Third World*. Princeton, NJ: Princeton University Press.

81. Dennis A. Rondinelli. 1982. The Dilemma of Development Administration: Complexity and Uncertainty in Control-Oriented Bureaucracies. *World Politics*, Vol. 35, No. 1.

82. Ma Concepcion P. Alfiler. 1983. P. 35.

83. M. P. Cracknell and J. H. Feingold. 1982. Including the Marginal Producer. *CERES*, May-June 1982, p. 16.

84. G. Shabbir Cheema and Dennis A. Rondinelli. 1983. Decentralization and Development: Conclusions and Directions. *In* G. Shabbir Cheema and Dennis A. Rondinelli. 1983. Pp. 295-315.

85. David D. Gow and Jerry VanSant. 1981. P. 6.

86. George H. Honadle and David D. Gow. 1981. *Putting the Cart Behind the Horse: Participation, Decentralization, and Capacity Building for Rural Development*. Washington DC: Development Alternatives, Inc.

87. Janice Jiggins. 1977. Motivation and Performance of Extension Field Staff. *In* ODI. 1977. *Extension, Planning, and the Poor*. London: Overseas Development Institute, Agriculture Administration Unit, Occasional Paper 2.

88. John Howell. 1981. *Administering Agricultural Development for Small Farmers*. Rome: FAO of the UN.

89. A. N. Seth. 1977. *Organizing the Rural Poor for Integrated Rural Development: Problems and Prospects*. Bangalore: Asian Institute for Rural Development (mimeo). P. 33. Also see, S. M. Pandey (ed.). 1976. *Rural Labour in India*. New Delhi: Shri Ram Centre for Industrial Relations and Human Resources.

90. D. C. Korten and N. T. Uphoff. 1981. *Bureaucratic Reorientation for Rural Development*. Manila: Asian Institute of Management/Ithaca, NY: Cornell University, Rural Development Committee.

91. Gloria Davis. 1981. *Promoting Increased Food Production in the 1980s*. Proceedings of the Second Annual Agricultural Sector Symposium, 5-9 January 1981., Washington DC: The World Bank. Quoted from Michael M. Cernea. 1983.

92. Gerrit Huizer. 1983. *Guiding Principles for People's Participation Projects*. Rome: FAO of the UN. Also see, Bernard Van Heck. 1979. *Research Guidelines for Field Action Projects to Promote Participation of the Poor in Rural Organizations*. Rome: FAO of the UN.

93. David D. Gow and Jerry VanSant. 1981. P. 11.

94. Michael M. Cernea. 1983. P. 65.

95. F.B. Alfonso, G.A. Mendoza and B.C. Bagadion Jr. 1983. *Empowering Rural Communities*. Manila: Asian Institute of Technology (mimeo).

96. H. D. Siebel and A. Massing. 1974. *Traditional Organizations and Economic Development: Studies of Indigenous Organizations in Liberia.* New York: Praeger.
97. Milton J. Easman and John D. Montgomery. 1980. The Administration of Human Development. *In* Peter T. Knight (ed.). 1980. *Implementing Programs of Human Development.* Washington DC: The World Bank (Staff Working Paper No. 403). Pp. 183-234.
98. Michael M. Cernea. 1981. Modernization and Development Potential of Traditional Grass-Roots Peasant Organizations. *In* M. O. Attir, B. Holzner, and Z. Suda (eds.). 1981. *Directions of Change: Modernization Theory, Research and Realities.* Boulder, Colo.: Westview Press.
99. Edward H. Spicer (ed.). 1952. *Human Problems in Technological Change.* New York: Russell Sage Foundation.
100. UNDP. 1979. *Rural Development* (Evaluation Study No. 2). New York: United Nations Development Programme, p. 33. Also see, J. Galvez Tan. 1985. Notes on Participatory Technology Development: *IFDA Dossier,* 45, January-February 1985, pp. 12-18.
101. Michael M. Cernea. 1983. P. 13.
102. World Bank. 1983. *Focus on Poverty: A Report by a Task Force of the World Bank.* Washington DC: The World Bank. P. 15.
103. Coralie Bryant and Louise G. White. 1982. *Managing Development in the Third World.* Boulder, Colo.: Westview Press. Chapter 10, Managing Participation, 212-13.
104. David D. Gow and Jerry VanSant. 1981. P. 9.
105. C. F. Sweet and P. F. Waisel. 1979. Process Versus Blueprint Models for Designing Rural Development Projects. *In* G. Honadle and Rudi Klauss. 1979.
106. David D. Gow and Jerry VanSant. 1981. Pp. 9-10.
107. Milton J. Easman. 1983. *Public Administration and Rural Development in ASEAN Countries.* Paper for the Colloquium on Administration of Rural Development in ASEAN Countries, Jakarta, 5-13 September 1983. Organised by the UN Economic and Social Commission for Asia and the Pacific. P. 2.
108. US Agency for International Development. 1980. *Problems in Implementing the Integrated Development Project in Liberia.* Audit Report 80-82.
109. Hari Mohan Mathur. 1983. *Improving the Performance of Agricultural Development Administration.* Paper presented at the Global Expert Consultation on Organization and Management Structures for Rural Development: Agricultural Services to Small Farmers. Italy, 12-15 December 1983. Organised by FAO of the UN. Also see, David D. Kortan. 1984. Strategic-Organization for People-Centered Development. *Public Administration Review,* Vol. 44, No. 4, July-August 1984, 341-52.
110. D. W. Brinkerhoff. 1979. Inside Public Bureaucracy: Empowering Managers to Empower Clients. *Rural Development Participation Review,* 1(1). Also see, United Nations. 1983. *Enhancing Capabilities for Administrative Reform in Developing Countries.* New York: UN DTDC.
111. FAO. 1984. *Motivation of Public Officials Serving Small Farmers: The Asian Context.* Rome: FAO of the UN.
112. Samuel Paul. 1983. *Training for Public Administration and Management in Developing Countries: A Review.* Washington DC. The World Bank (Staff Working Paper No. 584).

113. Norman Uphoff. 1981. Farmers' Participation in Project Formulation, Design, and Operation. *Promoting Increased Food Production in the 1980s.* Proceedings of the Second Annual Agricultural Sector Symposium, 5-9 January 1981. Washington DC: The World Bank. P. 274. Quoted here from Michael M. Cernea. 1983.

114. World Bank. 1983. *World Development Report, 1983.* New York: Oxford University Press. P. 92.

115. Samuel Paul. 1982. *Managing Development Programs: The Lessons of Success.* Boulder, Colo.: Westview Press.

116. World Bank. 1980. *World Development Report, 1980.* Washington DC: The World Bank. P. 81.

Reaching the Poor in Rural Areas

In development plans of most Third World countries the program-mes specially focused on the rural poor did not figure prominently enough until very recently.[1] The financial institutions have a long history of being opposed to investments in rural development projects which had to be defended from the criticism that they were nothing but 'handoutism'.[2] In fact, economists never thought much of small farmers as producers. 'They aren't the real "producers"; they eat practically everything they raise, they are largely outside the money economy, and they add very little to the country's wealth.'[3] So ran their usual line of arguments.

On the other hand, many economists in the past genuinely thought that to step up agricultural production by supporting rich farmers on their large, modern farms was the best way of ushering in the 'Green Revolution'. Further, they believed that once the development process thus gained some ground, the condition of the poor was bound to change for the better through its spin-off effects.[4]

The rural poor — inarticulate, unorganised, stratified and dispersed — could not have been in a position to demand their due specially in the face of such prevailing views which were wholly unfavourable to them. Indeed, there are some observers who now clearly see an urban bias in much of the development planning as practised in the Third World.[5] And it is to this factor that they attribute the persisting poverty in rural areas.

The Significance of Small Farmers

However, the past few years have witnessed a sea-change in the attitude towards small farmers.[6] Small farmers are no longer regarded as economically unviable.[7] Rather, their significance is coming to be more widely recognised. Compared to large farmers, the small farmers are undoubtedly in a disadvantageous position on several counts. But they also enjoy certain advantages which are unique to them. A recent World Bank document highlighted some of the characteristics of small farms which appear to make them competitive than larger farms:

> Small farmers are unable to exploit economies of scale. Their transaction costs are high because their marketed output, purchases of inputs, and use of credit are on a small-scale.
> Lack of assets limits their ability to borrow money; land is often rented and cannot be used as collateral.
> Small farmers cannot afford to spend as much as large farmers to explore and adopt new techniques. Productivity gains from new techniques usually increase profits among those who use them first.
> Small farmers tend to be the first to suffer during shortages of fertiliser, seed, and water. They lack the influence exerted by their larger neighbours, whose goodwill is more important to local suppliers.[8]

However, the advantages which small farms enjoy are by no means inconsiderable. Continuing, the report adds:

> Offsetting factors are that small farmers benefit from lower labour costs and self-management.... The quality of farming is even more important than its cost. Farming is a complicated business that requires not only hard work but also care and attention. The small farmer's motivation is usually strong, especially if he is growing food to feed the family. Small farmers exploit their advantages (and offset some of their disadvantages) by putting more hours of work into each hectare than large farmers do.[9]

The arguments of economic viability have been an important factor in winning the support of planners in favour of poverty-focused rural development programmes. Compared to the urban setting, the rural setting is less likely to induce planners to do things for the poor automatically. In an insightful World Bank paper, Judith Tendler observes:

The density and isolation of the poor in cities then, creates the need for certain projects that are highly apt for targetting on the poor and, at the same time, are attractive to donors. In rural areas, in contrast, these same infrastructure projects seem to represent the worst of all worlds. They have no chance of financial self-sufficiency; they are costly per user served or per unit of facility produced; their benefits are reaped at least as much by the rich as by the poor; and they cannot fall back — like the urban projects can — on the support of an implicit equity justification. The spatial dispersion of the rural poor, in other words, limits markedly the possible choices of projects for them.[10]

More and more evidence is now coming in from various places to confirm that it would be sound economics to pursue the anti-poverty programmes. Writing on India, Pran Chopra emphatically observes:

... In the last five years or so, a cluster of social and economic experiments scattered across India have demonstrated that it is cheaper to remove poverty than to let it persist. Though not yet widely shared, this perception is supported by field experience indicating that poverty is much less massive than hitherto believed. Moreover, the benefits of removing it may be calculated not only in social and humanitarian terms but purely in the economic sense as well. Poverty, it has now been shown, can be removed by means that recover their costs in fairly short periods of time.[11]

During the past ten years the wide support which development programmes aimed at the alleviation of rural poverty have won appears to be fairly impressive. As a theme for research from various disciplinary perspectives, as an agenda for discussion in conferences and as a focal point for action projects on the ground, rural poverty today has few rivals of equal attractiveness.[12] Problems of the poor have come on to the centre stage in a dominant position from the hiding as it were.

Equity considerations, and the fact that past development pursuits led to a worsening of the condition of the poor, while the rich did better as never before, are among the factors that have considerably influenced the policy options.[13] Persistence of poverty on a large-scale does not speak well of state interventions to ameliorate the situation. Failure on this front in a conspicuous way is something which governments are most apprehensive about. Sooner or later such failures could not only erode their support bases among the rural poor who are in a clear numerical majority, but also add to social tensions and other problems of day-to-day governmental management of public affairs. The poor are likely to remain around for quite some time to come. Possibilities of a sharp decline in their numbers in the near future seem rather dim.[14]

Indeed, the poor can no longer be ignored.[15] Providing developmental assistance to the rural poor is now emerging as a matter of great concern to planning agencies and development experts everywhere.[16] The World Conference on Agrarian Reform and Rural Development (WCARRD) convened by the FAO in Rome in 1979 adopted a Programme of Action which particularly emphasised the need to establish and strengthen institutions for the delivery of inputs and services with the direct involvement of organised groups of small farmers and other groups of rural poor in order to ensure equitable access.[17]

Public Services and Participation

To serve the poor a fairly intricate network of public services has now come into existence.[18] This build-up not only seeks to promote the productive, especially income-generating, capability of the poor but also hopes to meet their basic needs. The basic needs approach is commended on the ground that, while meeting urgent human needs for food, clothing, health, shelter, etc., it eventually contributes to the raising of productivity. Regarded as significant in the long-run, the impact of this approach is not intangible even in the short-run.[19] Public services designed to promote productivity include extension services, agricultural inputs distribution, credit, irrigation, roads, and marketing centres. Programmes set up to provide schooling, health services and potable water fall into the category of public services meant to improve the quality of life.

Other approaches to reaching the poor view their involvement in the development process as of crucial significance.[20] Obviously participation has some definite advantages.[21] The developmental needs of the people become better known and based on needs determined this way the development agencies can then proceed to plan and administer programmes in a more realistic manner, in a way that people will find them acceptable. Once the people become aware of what the government is doing for them, they voluntarily come forward to seek the services. Their demand, then, keeps the local level officials on the alert. In fact, they can help the local officials to accomplish many development tasks for them.

However, unless the people themselves are ready to receive what the government agencies are there to provide, development will not occur as planned. It is, therefore, important that the receiving systems be developed alongside the delivery systems.[22] Participation of the poor and their organisations is of critical significance to the entire plan of reaching them and promoting their development.

However, participation is nowhere achieved easily.[23] More frequently, it is the affluent groups that come out and not the poor for whom the plans are really meant. The poor are in no position to incur the wrath of the elites on whom their dependence is near total. The rich are much too strong to let the poor get away with benefits that development brings on the village scene. Participatory local organisations tend to be dominated by the elites and thus do little to provide opportunities for effective participation by the poor.[24]

Organising the poor is commended as a way of making them more vociferous in articulating their demand on the development agencies and the others concerned and thus enhancing their bargaining power overall. This can facilitate their getting inputs, credit and better prices for what they produce.[25] Caroll P Streeter has underlined the importance of organisation '... the small farmers of the world ... will sooner or later have to stop attempting singlehandedly to cope with an organized world. The contest is too uneven.'[26]

There cannot be anything objectionable in the rural poor coming together on a common platform to seek their advancement along lines that governments themselves are keen to promote. However, it is not easy to create organisations of the poor. People in villages do not all think alike and act alike. Their interests and the manner in which they wish to pursue them are often quite divergent. Where income differences do not divide the people, caste considerations do, as in the villages of India. Communication barriers are formidable indeed.[27]

Target Group Planning

Providing services to the rural poor continues to be regarded as an effective way of promoting their development.[28] To ensure that public services meant for the poor reach them intact, many projects have sought to make a direct attack on poverty. Identifying the clusters where the poor are concentrated and channelling the project benefits to them exclusively sounds an ideal strategy.[29] In any case, the development needs of the poor and the affluent are not the same.[30]

In practice, the target group approach does not seem to work out so well. Concentration of development efforts on the poorer groups arouses the hostility of the elites who then muster their resources to make sure that the project implementation does not proceed as planned. Erik Eckholm cites an example from Ethiopia:

> ... even direct efforts to aid the poor can backfire. A program to boost crop output in a fertile province of Ethiopia, initiated by the Swedish aid agency ... had nightmarish results.... The donors concentrated their aid among tenants and small farmers in the hope of improving their incomes directly. The program quite successfully increased production, but in the end the target groups were hurt rather than helped. Seeing how lucrative modern agriculture could be, landowners evicted thousands of tenants and began purchasing tractors. For the remaining tenants rents were raised from one-third of their crops to one half, so that the landlords gained proportionately more from any progress. As land prices doubled, any hope that [the] tenants might be able to purchase the lands they worked disappeared.[31]

Such experiences have led some observers to suggest caution in proceeding with programmes designed exclusively for the poor. Arousing hostility of the elites certainly will not be in the best interests of the poorer groups which these programmes aim to promote. It was recently noted that, if target group planning is to succeed 'a one-way approach of concentrating on the development of the poorer sections alone will not help. The elites must also be simultaneously targeted for attitudinal transformation so that they become willing partners in a development process skewed in favour of the poor.'[32] But a more practical suggestion would be to ensure that the new rural development projects also 'include something in them for their potential opponents, the rural elites. This may neutralize their opposition, and perhaps enlist their power in support of the project.'[33]

The Impact of Anti-Poverty Programmes

Programmes for the poor have been in operation now for the past several years. The question is: in terms of the impact on poverty alleviation, what exactly has been the contribution of governmental efforts to improve access of the poor to public services? This is an important question to consider.

Evaluation studies are increasingly reaching the conclusion that public services designed to serve the poor have largely remained beyond their reach.[34] Through a series of field workshops in several Asian countries, the FAO studied this problem in its regional project — ASARRD (Asian Survey of Agrarian Reform and Rural Development) — undertaken with the assistance of the UNDP. The findings of these field workshops, which confirm the results of similar studies in Asia and elsewhere, are succinctly summarised in a paper recently prepared by G Cameron Clark. Excerpted from this paper, the following findings from ASARRD graphically depict what actually has been happening on the ground.[35]

1. The vast majority of the rural poor were not being reached by existing programmes. Most of the farmer participants in the field workshops previously had no opportunity to meet government staff. Clearly, the 'delivery system' of government departments was not reaching this sector.
2. Few of the small farmers were even aware of the government programmes and most of those who did know about a specific programme felt either the recommended practices were irrelevant to their poor conditions or that they were not eligible to participate. Many thought that the government extension services were meant only for a few of the more important people in the village.
3. Few were members of village institutions such as cooperatives and even fewer actively participated in their activities.
4. Most of the rural poor needed credit and were heavily indebted

to local money-lenders or richer relatives. Few had made an attempt to get institutional credit as they felt they were both ineligible due to lack of collateral, and inadequate, due to illiteracy and their general social position.

5. National banks were under pressure from most governments to increase their loans to the rural sector but found it increasingly difficult to find bankable rural clients.

6. Most government extension staff were relying on the progressive farmers to disseminate improved practices to the rural poor. They were blindly following the trickle-down theory of development.

7. Every country had one or more pilot rural development programmes which were successful in the early stages but either failed when the original, highly motivated, project staff were withdrawn or failed to become self-reliant due to the paternalistic project staff who made themselves indispensable to the continuation of the project. This applied equally to projects initiated by government, international or bilateral aid agencies or non-governmental organisations.

8. Few development programmes were suitable for helping the landless agricultural labourers, the small fishermen or the women and youth of poor families to gain greater self-reliance and increased incomes.

9. Most programmes were planned from the top with very limited consultation with either the field staff or the farmers themselves, particularly the small farmers and peasants. There was almost no awareness amongst the government staff of the importance of people's participation in plan formulation and evaluation.

10. Because of their limited resources and inability to take risks, small farmers, tenants and landless agricultural labourers had priorities very different from those of the bigger farmers. Despite this, research programmes were concentrating their attention almost exclusively on crop and livestock production for farmers with assured irrigation and modern facilities. Technology appropriate to the poor, such as for rainfed agriculture, was receiving virtually no attention.

11. Area development programmes, including those being implemented with the assistance of international agencies were neglecting the distinctive needs for the low-income

disadvantaged families. It was taken for granted that some-how the programmes would carry the benefits to all people in the area, including the disadvantaged even when they consti-tuted the vast majority.

12. The status and condition of the small farmers and peasants were rapidly declining from owner-farmer to part-owner, part-tenant, share-cropper and eventually to labourer. At the same time the income of farmers with access to new technology, inputs and services was increasing, resulting in a rapid widening of the gap in the rural areas between the rich and the poor.

13. It was observed that there was now emerging in the rural areas a middle-level entrepreneur class of farmers who were generally less mindful of the interests and welfare of the small farmers and landless than the earlier, paternalistic landlord class. The competition between this modern sector farmer, who has access to capital and skills, and the poor peasant farmer is increasing with devastating results for the weak and the poor.

14. The link between land reform and agricultural development programmes was generally very weak resulting in limited co-relation between improved land reform measures and increased production.

15. Most agricultural and rural development programmes were concentrating their resources on strengthening the capacity of the different line departments of government, which forms its 'delivery system,' to deliver their inputs and ser-vices to the rural people in general. Almost no attention was being given to developing a better understanding amongst staff of the need to reach the disadvantaged, low-income sec-tor or in helping this sector to improve its capacity to com-pete for, receive and utilize these inputs and services. In all the countries, only one or two programmes were identified in which the rural poor were being actively assisted to develop their own 'receiving/utilizing system' as a means of gaining better access to the inputs and services available, theoretically to all, through the 'delivery system' of gov-ernment departments and agencies. It was repeatedly observed that the more educated and influential farmers possessed their own built-in 'receiving/utilizing system'

through direct contacts with government workers and through control of the local socio-economic institutions such as local government, the cooperative and production and marketing associations.

Partly, the disappointing results from the people-centred development approaches should be traceable to the fact that they really have not been pursued seriously enough. The methods adopted to involve the poor in development programmes have been rather uninspiring, one such method has been described by Edgar Owens:

> Commonly a civil servant asks a group of farmers to organize a cooperative in a village with little or no discussion of the possible advantages for a farmer member or how a cooperative ought to be organized and managed. Long accustomed to respond affirmatively to government suggestions, the farmers agree, have their names entered on the membership role, and elect officers. The president is invariably either a person of status in the local community or an individual who serves as the agent of a person of status. Many a village cooperative has been organized in this fashion in the course of a morning or an afternoon.[36]

Bureaucracy and the Poor

In its decisions, procedures and actions, the rural poor do not seem to matter much to the bureaucracy; it is still quite common to consider them last of all. The poor continue to be viewed as passive recipients of benefits from development projects and not as participants in the real sense of the term. Obviously, this must change if participatory methods are to realise their goal of promoting development of the rural poor at an accelerated pace.

Indeed, in reaching its real clients, the record of public services has remained rather dismal.[37] Why should that be so? What can be done to improve the administration of public services for the rural poor? These are some of the questions that are troubling governments and international development agencies alike.

The fact of the matter is that methods of administration that yield satisfactory results in one situation prove quite unworkable in another. No one knows for sure what works and what does not. In this context, Warren C Baum noted, 'Our experience todate has not yielded any ready made solutions for putting together an institution which can effectively and economically deliver goods and services to large numbers of people — who are often in remote areas and outside the ordinary ambit of government....'[38] To a remark by Julius Nyerere that while the United States was making an attempt to reach the moon, Tanzania was striving to reach its villages, David K Leonard rightly added: 'It appears that Tanzania had the harder task and one more critical for development.'[39] By its very nature promoting development of the rural poor cannot be an easy task.

Some of the failures of the public services in reaching the targeted poor groups arise from the way the bureaucracies are organised and operate.[40] The inherent limitations of a bureaucratic approach need to be understood properly. Regulatory functions are what the bureaucracies were established to perform. Even today they are able to handle these functions fairly adequately in normal circumstances, and quite creditably in special situations. Meeting emergencies like floods, droughts, and holding elections on a scale as large as in India are not small operations. Promoting development of the poor is, however, not a regulatory function.

The conduct of development operations is hindered by such characteristic features of the bureaucracy as lack of accountability, absence of incentives, long decision-making processes, overstaffing, hierarchy, rigidity, maintenance of status quo, conservatism, and lack of innovative approaches.[41] In the bureaucratic system there is no place for clients who, in this case, are the rural poor. Unlike private organisations where feedback on performance is instantly reflected in the volume of sales and margins of profit/loss, and where performance consistently counts for survival, public organisations are under no such pressures to maintain their performance at certain levels. They also lack quick methods to obtain feedback on their operations. Whether or not the poor are served as intended does not affect them at all. There are thus no compulsions to do better.

Some of the constraints under which the administrators function at the local level, where they really come in contact with the rural poor, are discussed here:

1. Expansion which bureaucracies have witnessed everywhere seems not to have occurred on the village scene. In relation to

the task, the number of extension workers remains pitifully small in most countries of the Third World. Some data on this aspect which has recently become available from Africa is illuminating. The ratio of extension workers to farmers is 1:2000 in Ethiopia, 1:2200 in Nigeria and 1:500 in Tanzania.[42] Comparing the situation in developed and developing countries, Jonathan Power and Anne-Marie Holstein note: 'In the developed countries the ratio of government agricultural agents to farm families is about 1:400. In developing countries it averages 1:8000....'[43] In Third World countries where people are still steeped in illiteracy and, therefore, hard to reach through modern media, especially the printed word, surely there is a need for more extension workers.

2. There is not only a shortage of personnel at the lower levels, where this may prove to be a critical factor in serving the rural poor, but the quality of personnel is not what it should be. The personnel is just not equipped to face the challenges of a changing rural scene. Field postings have lost the prestige they once enjoyed, and instead the career conscious civil servants now invariably look to their postings in the capital city, closer to their peers and centres of authority. With regard to extension agents Jedlicka neatly sums up the existing position '... extension jobs are often low-paid, non-prestigious, overworked occupations performed by ill-trained, poorly motivated people who therefore virtually insure the failure of any effort....'[44] Low salaries and other deteriorating working conditions are beginning to turn away many from the public service.

3. The officials on field jobs do not get opportunities to stay at one place for a certain minimum period. The turnover rate is quite extraordinary. Even before they begin to understand the nature of the assignment, orders come for their transfer to some other unfamiliar place. In implementing programmes for the poor, the officials sometimes run into difficulties with the rural elites because those programmes upset the status quo. And the elites, in turn, immediately pull strings to secure the transfer order. Officers who lack pliability are discovering to their dismay that they cannot function in a really straightforward manner to implement the poverty-focused programmes. Indeed, many officials are beginning to think that it is

prudent not to be enthusiastic about the government prog-rammes. If such conditions are allowed to develop further, implementation of development programmes for the poor is unlikely to proceed as intended.

The officials who do well are often not liked by the local elites. Even when their interests are not hurt, the local elites do not feel very happy with the good work done by an honest official. On the basis of his performance a good officer surely gains some popularity which they think is at their expense. The replacement becomes necessary simply because his work happens to be good. Thus, there has been some premium on the poor performers, and of late this uptrend has gained quite a momentum. And the performance of many a programme in the rural areas has begun deteriorating under the stewardship of officials of an indifferent calibre.

4. Differences in urban and rural environments are rather strik-ing in most Third World countries. The gulf between the urban and rural worlds is not narrowing down; it is widening. Most administrators still come from an urban background, and they really find it hard to adjust to the living conditions in rural areas. Doing something for the rural poor may be suffi-cient motivation for many to seek a field assignment, but the families surely need better health care, educational facilities, etc., which are available only in urban localities. Salaries are too low, and officials cannot afford to send their children to educational institutions in the cities.

   The urban background of the administrators also comes in the way of their seeing the rural problems through the eyes of the rural poor. Planners know even less about the socio-cul-tural context of development problems in tradition-bound rural societies.[45] Many projects end up in failure simply because of ignorance concerning village life. Contacts with the poorer groups are infrequent mainly because there is very little in common between the officials and the people whom they are supposed to serve. Past memories of contacts with government agents do not encourage many to come forward to seek public services.

5. In considering the issues related to public services for the rural poor, most people tend to blame the local level officials for all failures in supplies not reaching their destination on time, in

the quantity required, and at a price fair enough even for the poorest. However, it must be remembered that here the administrative problems are not the only ones to be solved. The supplies are limited, and the demand is fast expanding. Howsoever efficient an administrative system might be, it cannot hope to deliver goods and services in limited supply to everybody. The local level officials, then, depend on getting the supplies from outside, and if there are delays and prices are not right, there is really not much they can do.

6. Local level officials work in a set-up where all authority is concentrated at highest levels in the Central Government, delegation is virtually non-existent, and communication is only the top-down kind. They have responsibilities for the job but no powers to act. Even in minor matters, they must get decisions from top echelons in the government. Decision-making is a long, tortuous process in the highly centralised bureaucratic set-up. Inconsequential cases are subjected to a thorough examination from various viewpoints in, not one but, several ministries. By the time the decision is handed down to the officials at the operating level, there remains no need for that decision. The pressing urgency of the local level problems is often beyond the comprehension of those who are far from the scene. Yet it is extremely important that

> ... if a program is to win the trust of the people whom it hopes to serve, it has to deliver, and fast, all that it promises. If a field officer says that a truckload of cement will be available next Wednesday, it had better to be on hand at least by the following Monday, or villagers will have lost faith in the field officer, and will sink back into mistrust and apathy. So from the psychological point of view, efficient delivery of service from above is indispensable to a rapidly expanding operation.[46]

Despite delays in getting directions from above, the officials at local levels prefer not to go forward unless the signal comes first. To wait rather than to act is always safer. Administration of programmes for the poor is slowed down only because of this procedural rigidity. A farmer needing credit urgently will go to the local money-lender rather than wait indefinitely the arrival of some clarification from head-quarters on a reference made by the field official.

7. The process of planned development has led to the establishment of many new organisations and agencies. Indeed, there is always a temptation to establish new organisations whenever any new problem in the field comes to notice. Often more agencies than one are concerned with just one kind of service. Donor agencies themselves add to this proliferation by their preference for separate project organisations. The existence of numerous agencies in the field, sometimes performing very similar functions, creates horrendous coordination problems. Each agency zealously guards its position and tends to operate in rivalry with the other. In such a situation the multi-disciplinary dimension of the development process all but recedes into the background.

All this only makes things more difficult for the small farmer who cannot easily get what he needs because none of the services is a subject of exclusive concern to any one particular agency. Usually several agencies must agree before he can hope to get credit to buy seeds in time for sowing. Therefore, in his own interest, the farmer has to run from agency to agency only because they lack a system of working in cooperation with one another. An Asian Development Bank paper recently described this situation in the following words: 'With a multiplicity of agencies and departments each delivering their own particular input for development, and each operating relatively independently of the other, it is often the end-user (usually the small farmer) who, de facto, has to act as the coordinator of these activities.'[47]

8. Often the field level officials are drafted for short periods to do various administrative jobs quite unconnected with their own. And these jobs take precedence over their departmental work. Duty at the polling booths becomes a matter of overriding priority during election days. Then, the most important duty of the irrigation engineer is to see that he functions properly as presiding officer at an election booth miles away from his headquarters. It does not matter if even the standing crops are destroyed simply because he is unable to run the canals at this time.

And, then, a task that is considered important at one time

gets relegated to the background another time. Other more pressing tasks emerge. When there are no elections, there is the family planning campaign, or the savings mobilisation drive or the school enrolment week, etc. Frequent assignments of this nature divert the attention of field level officials from their real task of serving the poor. This also creates in their minds uncertainties as to what exactly the priorities of the government are in pursuing so many diverse activities.

From the foregoing it would appear that bureaucracies as they are and as they function in most Third World countries are in no position to implement effectively the poverty-focused rural development programmes. But the solution does not lie in eliminating the bureaucracy.[48] Of course, changes need to be effected in the administrative system to make it more responsive to the aspirations of the poor. The following statement affirms the significant role of administration:

> This emphasis on constituency organizations does not challenge or contradict more orthodox concerns with improving the effectiveness of administrative operations. It does not hold that government administrators are exploiters or that their elimination is required in order to return power to the people. Nor does it deny the importance of bureaucratic leadership or of creative initiative in development administration.[49]

Improving Administrative Performance

Administration for development is beginning to attract attention not only of governments responsible for the fate of masses of their poor, but also of international development agencies who now see no great chance for their projects making a dent on the poverty situation unless organisations capable of implementing the projects as planned are first set up on the ground. It is in recognition of the significance of administrative dimension in the development process that Management of Development was the theme selected for the 1983 World Development Report.[50] Development administration experts are still not associated during the appraisal of bank-aided projects etc., but such a role is bound to emerge sooner or later.

The search for innovative ways of improving the administrative capability so as to make both planning and implementation systems better adapted to developmental needs of the rural poor have not yielded as yet any prescriptions which may be applicable to all situations everywhere anytime.[51] Indeed, the problems need to be further studied in depth, over time and in a variety of locations. Factors which lead to success and failure of development programmes are equally important to an understanding of the issues involved. However, it is the study of failures which seems to have attracted attention so far. More research effort needs to be now expended on the study of successful cases to correct the imbalance. Arguing that the lessons of success are far more important here, Samuel Paul in his recent thought-provoking book states emphatically:

> ... Undoubtedly there is much to learn from the experience of low performers. But, by and large, such studies are more useful in identifying the errors to be avoided than the positive approaches to be adopted. The removal of obstacles does not necessarily ensure performance. This is essentially true in the field of management and implementation which are action oriented by their very nature. There is considerable evidence to show that successful management interventions and practices cannot be deduced or predicted from an analysis of failures or poor performance. Innovative approaches stem from discontinuities and not linear projections. That is why the prescriptions derived from such studies often fail to offer adequate guidance for action. In understanding the nature of public management and developing insights for improving the performance of development programs, there is a strong case for investigating the experience of high performers.[52]

Of course, it is not possible to wait for solutions to emerge from researches which tend to follow a protracted course. In the meantime, whatever has been learnt from studies and experience should be put to the best use possible. The situations confronting administrators in the field demand action now and here. Among the essential requirements for success in administering development programmes directed at the rural poor, the following appear to be particularly noteworthy.

1. The first thing which administrators need to appreciate is that programmes for the poor cannot be administered by following

the traditional bureaucratic approaches. Serving the rural poor is a developmental function, quite unlike the maintenance of law and order and collection of taxes. Not only should the administrators be prepared to learn and apply to these programmes the methods and techniques of modern management in place of outdated, antiquated, quaint administrative procedures, but should also imbibe a new set of attitudes towards the people whom they are meant to serve. They must learn not only to work for, but work with them.[53]

2. It is, then, important to realise that governmental agencies by themselves will not be able to accomplish the task. The task is much too big for them and also the problems to be addressed are of a kind different from those encountered in the past. The administrators must, therefore, discover ways of locating, supporting and using the organisations, the personnel, the procedures, and the resources other than the established governmental ones. The idea is to obtain better results at the least cost of time and money. To quote Montgomery:

> Perhaps the greatest role bureaucracies can play is to find ways of extending their own reach: to recruit, train, supervise, and deploy paraprofessionals, and to use their knowledge of legal requirements for the management of public resources; to mobilize local self-help efforts in the urban and rural slums; to improve the efficiency and effectiveness of voluntary groups willing to work with the poor; and, most important of all, to help organizations that already exist among the poor, giving them guidance in their own internal management, arbitrating among rival claimants when necessary, and providing them with information about the resources that might be available for their own further development. They can also act as links between these informal organizations in the field and the political and administrative leadership at the centre, to the benefit of both.[54]

3. The programmes need to be followed with single-minded determination and the administration has to be fully geared to achieve the set targets. It is, therefore, important that development goals be first defined in the clearest possible

terms, and resources required for their achievement be provided in full measure. On this need for specificity in spelling out the objectives, the *World Development Report 1978* noted:

> If more progress is to be made in alleviating poverty, it is essential that objectives be defined so that governments can monitor them regularly. Large amounts of resources and energy can be dissipated if operational clarity is lacking about targets, designs, and plans for the execution of poverty programs. Without such clarity, it is difficult either to assign administrative responsibility for implementation or to evaluate the effectiveness of different approaches to poverty alleviation, and impossible to learn from experience.[55]

The existence of such gaps in the process of development planning has recently been reported in a FAO document:

> Few countries have defined separate objectives and quantified targets for rural development, including poverty alleviation, within the framework of national development plans.
>
> Even fewer countries have separate rural development strategies or poverty alleviation strategies, combining policies, programmes and projects to make them operational with quantifiable targets for poverty reduction stated within the framework of their national plans.
>
> It has been found that data on income, undernutrition, land tenure, and land distribution constraints on agricultural production, people's participation and women in development, are not adequate to identify target groups of rural poor.
>
> Few countries collect data to make periodic evaluations of progress in rural poverty alleviation within the period of a development plan in order to adjust its policies and programmes.
>
> Few countries draw up an end-of-plan evaluation of progress in rural development and poverty alleviation or use such evaluations for setting rural development objectives in subsequent plans.[56]

Obviously issues involved in planning development of the poor, particularly aspects of planning related to administration, need to be given greater attention than has been the case till now.

4. Emphasis on procedures should give place to emphasis on achievement of results. The performance of officials should be judged on the basis of results produced, and not their skill in designing and pursuing procedures which only tend to kill the projects. It must be realised that minor errors can occur in achieving quick results. The insistence on zero-error observance of complicated, irrelevant, time-consuming rules will only lead to total inaction. If the existing procedures come in the way of speedy action, they must be scrutinised with a view to discarding them in favour of simpler ones that help promote rapid positive action. The rules should enable action to be taken promptly, and not to slow down the process.[57]

5. Continuous efforts are necessary to decentralise authority to lower levels of administration which are directly involved in plan implementation. It is officials at operating levels who must have the authority to make decisions on the spot. It must also be ensured that they do exercise the delegated authority.[58] There are some who think that officials at the field level are incapable of acting on their own. This may not be correct. Indeed, they are well placed in the field to perceive things as they are, and also to apply solutions that alone can set the problems right. The officials at the field level must be given a chance to work independently to some extent, and their capability for such action must be improved. Overcentralisation not only impedes speedy execution of projects, but also needlessly adds to the volume of work at the higher levels. Top officials surely need more time to plan and organise, rather than get bogged down with cumbersome details of trivial matters which the field level officials can handle on their own. Surely, there are certain problems that can be best tackled at some central point. The need is to determine what functions can be performed in the best manner possible at the centre and what functions can easily be delegated to the lower levels.

6. Properly designed systems of monitoring, implementation, and evaluation must be installed. It is important to get feedback on the performance of programmes as they move along.

This enables modifications to be made in the mid-course, thus resulting in considerable savings in the long-run. Monitoring systems will also help top officials at the centre to remain fully informed on all matters connected with projects on the ground, thus further obviating the need for a highly centralised system of administration.

7. The lack of coordination among various agencies is proving to be a great hindrance in delivering project benefits to the rural poor. Coordination problems exist at all levels. The problem needs to be tackled on a systematic basis.[59] Effective coordination needs to be introduced in the working of ministries and departments at the centre on the one hand, and among their agencies at various levels down the line right up to the village level, on the other. Improvements are also needed in coordination arrangements as they exist among agencies at various levels which come under the control of the same ministry or department. As proliferation of agencies tends to make things worse, the tendency to establish new units must be strongly resisted.

8. Another problem area which requires urgent attention is personnel. Existing systems of recruitment, training, assignment, etc., need considerable adaptations to the new situation. Personnel for rural development must be selected on the basis of aptitude and background. Traditional approaches to training have done little to equip the personnel for their task. A recent publication of the FAO has summed up the tasks which training must accomplish:

Government personnel need training to be more responsive to the needs of the poor. These needs often go unperceived when senior officials fail to travel off the surfaced roads, or during the rainy season when food supplies are at their lowest, and health at its worst, or when, in their visits to villages, they associate only with the local elite. Training must alert administrators and grassroots workers to these dangers. It must teach them to seek out the poorer groups and investigate their needs and conditions, and not only to deal with people who already use services, but also to seek out those who do not use them and find out why, so that the services can be redesigned, if necessary, in a way that will enable the poor to use them more. Training of personnel must include skills in human relations that have usually been neglected, skills, for example, in communicating with local people and local participatory organizations, in stimulating a two-way flow of information, in listening to local viewpoints and not simply dictating solutions. Communications media such as local newsletters, video and radio programmes to which local people are encouraged to contribute can help in this sphere.[60]

Also, on considerations of work efficiency the frequent transfers are totally meaningless. These must not be carried out erratically as at present. There must be sufficient incentive to attract the right people for rural postings. Ways must be found to generate among the staff a commitment to project goals, if performance of the poverty-focused rural development programmes is to improve.[61] Suggesting that motivation is the 'ultimate' constraint, Richard Heaver says, 'Real commitment to project goals can produce results despite ill-conceived structures and untrained manpower; while poorly motivated managers will achieve little with the best of training and in the most appropriate of structures.'[62]

9. Not all that is required to involve the people in decision-making concerning their development has been seriously attempted everywhere.[63] Empirically it has been established that participation leads to greater success in the implementation of programmes for the poor. Unless the people have a say in what they want, they are unlikely to extend their support to the project. Top-down planning approaches have their limitations. Development from below can help produce the intended results. Strategies must be designed to secure the participation of target groups of poor in ways that do not arouse the hostility of the elites who then use all their might only to wreck the project.

10. If development programmes are to be pursued on a sustained basis, increased effort must be made to improve capability of the entire administrative system.[64] The project approach shows quick results in the short-run, but this does not contribute to strengthening of the overall administrative

system. This is possible only by pursuing what has come to be called the programme approach.

Pressures to show quick results have led to the concentration of efforts on projects to make them particularly effective at the cost of normal programme agencies. However, unless adequate administrative, managerial, and technical capabilities for development are created in the governmental system as a whole, the development task will continue to elude both planners and administrators as has been the case so far. As David C Korten observes:

> Excessive pressures for immediate results, as measured by goods and services delivered, drive.out attention to institution building and make it difficult to move beyond a relief and welfare approach to poverty; the distribution of food is a lot faster than teaching people how to grow it. A substantial bias toward *project* as contrasted to *program* funding compounds the problem.[65]

Continuing he adds:

> · The need is for an adaptive, bottom-up process of program and organizational development through which an adequate fit may be achieved between beneficiary needs, program output, and organizational competence. This calls not for more sophisticated skills in the preparation of detailed project plans, but rather for skills in building capacities for action through action.[66]

At present it is fashionable to blame administrators for anything that goes wrong with development programmes for the poor. The administrators and the administrative system which they operate must undeniably get a large share of this blame. However, it would not be fair to place the blame entirely on them. Development is a complex process. Success here is not dependent only on one factor. Finance plays a crucial role. Technology is also important. Development now takes place in a political milieu and, indeed, one important question that must be considered here concerns the commitment of ruling elites to poverty-focused development policies. Do they really favour change in the existing situation? Gunnar Myrdal and Dudley Seers recently answered this question: 'The aim of many ruling elites is not to relieve poverty; rather the contrary, to make sure that the incomes of the masses are kept low and social services restricted.'[67] If this really is the situation in the Third World, improvements in the efficiency of administrative operations alone are unlikely to help relieve rural poverty to any great extent.

NOTES AND REFERENCES

1. The terms 'rural poor' and 'small farmers' are used here interchangeably.
2. The World Bank lending for rural development projects really began only from the early 1970s. See, World Bank. 1975. *Rural Development (Sector Policy Paper)*. Washington DC: The World Bank.
3. Carroll P. Streeter. 1975. *Reaching the Developing World's Small Farmers*. New York: The Rockefeller Foundation. P. 1.
4. Guy Hunter. 1982. Approaches to Rural Development since Independence. *ODI Review*, No. 1, pp. 38-49.
5. Michael Lipton. 1977. *Why Poor People Stay Poor: Urban Bias in World Development*. Cambridge, Mass: Harvard University Press.
6. Eliot R. Morse. 1976. *Strategies for Small Farmer Development*. (2 volumes). Boulder, Colorado: Westview Press. Also see, Guy Hunter and Anthony Bottrall (eds.). 1974. *Serving the Small Farmer: Policy Choices in Indian Agriculture*. Hyderabad: National Institute of Community Development, and London: Overseas Development Institute.
7. Wyn F. Owen. The Significance of Small Farmers in Developing Countries. *In* Huntley H. Biggs and Ronald L. Tinnermeier (eds.). 1974 *Small Farm Agricultural Development Problems*. Fort Collins, Colorado: Colorado State University. Pp. 21-45.
8. World Bank. 1982. *World Development Report 1982*. New York: Oxford University Press. Pp. 81-82.
9. World Bank. 1982. *World Development Report 1982*. New York: Oxford University Press. P. 82.
10. Judith Tendler. 1982. *Rural Projects through Urban Eyes: An Interpretation of the World Bank's New Style Rural Development Projects*. Washington DC: The World Bank (Staff Working Paper No. 532). P. 17.
11. Pran Chopra. Take-off for Self-Help. *CERES*, May-June 1982, p. 21.
12. An example is the research project Delivery Systems for Rural Development recently completed by the National Institute of Rural Development. Hyderabad which was funded by the Government of India's Planning Commission. Improving Public Service Delivery Systems for the Rural Poor was the theme of a Working Party held in New Delhi during November 1979 under the auspices of the Government of India and the United Nations Economic and

Social Commission for Asia and the Pacific.

13. Hollis Chenery et al. 1974. *Redistribution With Growth.* New York: Oxford University Press.

14. FAO. 1982. Rural Poverty in Developing Countries and Means of Poverty Alleviation: World Review. *The State of Food and Agriculture 1981* (FAO Agriculture Series No. 14). Rome: FAO of the UN. Pp 78-79. It quotes from another FAO study, FAO. 1981. *Agriculture Towards 2000 AD.* Rome: FAO of the UN, in support of the projection that in 2000 AD the undernourished population is likely to exceed 400 million, only slightly less than in 1980. And this is considered an optimistic projection.

15. S.C. Varma. 1981. *India's Attack on Rural Poverty.* New Delhi: Government of India. Ministry of Rural Reconstruction.

16. Government of India. 1982. *Report of the Expert Group on Programmes for Alleviation of Poverty.* New Delhi: Planning Commission.

17. FAO. 1981. *The Declaration of Principles and Programme of Action of the World Conference on Agrarian Reform and Rural Development.* Rome: FAO of the UN. Pp. 18-19.

18. Welfare Programme of the Rural Poor. *Monthly Commentary on Indian Economic Condition,* 23 (5), December 1981, 109-14.

19. Paul Streeten et al. 1981. *First Things First: Meeting Basic Human Needs in Developing Countries.* New York: Oxford University Press.

20. John M. Cohen and Norman T. Uphoff. 1977. *Rural Development Participation.* Ithaca, New York: Cornell University, Centre for International Studies, Rural Development Monograph No. 2.

21. Max Millikan et al. 1969. *The Role of Popular Participation in Development.* Cambridge, Mass: The MIT Press. Also see, John D. Montgomery and Milton J. Easman. Popular Participation in Development Administration. *Journal of Comparative Administration,* 3:3, November 1971.

22. The need for grassroots receiving/utilising mechanisms has been especially emphasised in *Small Farmers Development Manual,* Vol. 1. 1978. Chapter 3. Bangkok: FAO of the UN, Regional Office.

23. William C. Thiensenhusen. Reaching the Rural Poor and the Poorest: A Goal Unmet. *In* Howard Newby (ed.). 1978. *International Perspectives in Rural Sociology.* New York: John Wiley & Sons.

24. Concerning participatory local organisations, research has accumulated evidence both to support the view that they help promote rural development and also that they provide little effective opportunity for participation. Supporting the first proposition are two significant studies: Norman T. Uphoff and Milton J. Easman. 1974. *Local Organizations for Rural Development: Analysis of Asian Experience.* Ithaca: Cornell University Press, Rural Development Committee; and Elliott R. Morss et al. 1975. *Strategies for Small Farmer Development: An Empirical Study of Rural Development Projects* (Executive Summary). Washington DC: Development Alternatives, Inc. See the following studies which support the other proposition: Samuel P. Huntington and Joan M. Nelson. 1976. *No Easy Choice: Political Participation in Developing Countries.* Cambridge, Mass: Harvard University Press. Pp. 134-57. UNRISD. 1975. *Rural Cooperatives as Agents of Change: A Research Report and a Debate.* Geneva: United Nations Research Institute for Social Development (Series on Rural Institutions and Planned Change No. 8).

25. M. P. Cracknell and J. H. Feingold. 1982. Including the Marginal Producer. *CERES*, May-June 1982, pp. 16-20.
26. Caroll P. Streeter. 1975. *Reaching the Developing World's Small Farmers*. New York: The Rockefeller Foundation. Pp. 46-47.
27. John W. Gartoll. 1981. Inequality within the Rural Communities of India. *American Sociological Review*, 46 (6), pp. 768-82. Also see, David C. Porter. 1981. The Politics of Poverty in Rural Asia (A Review Article). *Pacific Affairs*, 54 (3), pp. 502-9.
28. The term 'delivery' of services has a certain top-down implication. Yet in the circumstances there is no way of leaving the poor to themselves. See in this connection, FAO. 1982. *Delivery Systems in Support of the Small Farmer in Asia*. Rome: FAO of the UN. P. 3.
29. R. P. Misra. 1980. Target Groups and Regional Development. *Regional Development Dialogue*, Vol. I, Spring 1980, pp. 21-56. Also see, Reaching and Involving the Target Population. *In* DPMC. 1976. *Elements of Project Management*. Washington DC: Development Project Management Centre. Pp. 100-6.
30. A distinction between programme priorities for the whole community and for low-income, disadvantaged small farmers is neatly summarised in a table in ASARRD. 1977. *Starting From Below (Project Findings and Recommendations)*. Rome: FAO of the UN and UNDP. P. 8.
31. Erik Eckholm. 1979. *The Dispossessed of the Earth: Land Reform and Sustainable Development*. Washington DC: Worldwatch Institute (Worldwatch Paper No. 30). P. 36.
32. K. V. Sundaram. Comment on the paper by R. P. Misra. Target Groups and Regional Development: Case for a More Comprehensive Social Policy. *Regional Development Dialogue*, Vol. I, No. 1, Spring 1980, p. 48.
33. Judith Tendler. 1982. *Rural Projects through Urban Eyes: An Interpretation of the World Bank's New Style Rural Development Projects*. Washington DC: The World Bank (Staff Working Paper No. 532). P. 58.
34. Government of India. 1980. *Accessibility of the Poor to the Rural Water Supply: A Quick Evaluation Study (1978-79)*. New Delhi: Planning Commission, Programme Evaluation Organization.
35. G. Cameron Clark. 1982. *ASARRD and Small Farmers Development in Asia*. Bangkok: FAO Regional Office for Asia and the Pacific. Pp. 3-5.
36. Edgar Owens. 1976. Small Farmer Participation and World Agricultural Development. *Public Administration Review*, Vol. 36, No. 2, March-April 1976, p. 144.
37. V. S. Vyas. 1980. Missing Links in the Delivery System. *Kurukshetra*, 29 (1), 1 October 1980, pp. 52-56.
38. Warren C. Baum. 1978. The Project Cycle. *Finance and Development*, Vol. 15, No. 4, December 1978.
39. David K. Leonard. 1982. Analyzing the Organisational Requirements for Serving the Rural Poor. *In* David K. Leonard and Dale Rogers Marshall (eds.). 1982. *Institutions of Rural Development for the Poor: Decentralization and Organizational Linkages*. Berkeley: University of California, Institute of International Studies. P. 1.
40. Ram C. Malhotra. 1981. Some Issues in the Management of Integrated Rural Development. *Kalamana*, 2 (1 and 2), January-June 1981, 34-48. Also see,

David K. Leonard. 1977. *Reaching the Peasant Farmer: Organizational Theory and Practice in Kenya.* Chicago: University of Chicago Press.
41. Robert Chambers. 1974. *Managing Rural Development: Ideas and Experiences from East Africa.* Uppasala: Scandinavian Institute of African Studies. Also see, Amal Ray and Vanita Venkatasubhiah. 1982. Administrative Constraints on Rural Development. *Economic and Political Weekly,* Vol. XVII, No. 26, 26 June 1982, pp. A-63 to A-67.
42. S. Ramakrishnan. 1982. Issues on the Organization and Administration of Agricultural Services for Small Farmers in Africa. *In* FAO. 1982. *Improving the Organization and Administration of Agricultural Services for Small Farmers in Africa.* Report of a Regional Expert Consultation held in Nairobi, Kenya, December 1982. Rome: FAO of the UN. P. 38.
43. Jonathan Power and Anne-Marie Holstein. 1980. *World of Hunger: A Strategy for Survival.* London: Maurice Temple Smith Ltd. P. 113.
44. Allen D. Jedlicka. 1977. *Organization for Rural Development: Risk-taking and Appropriate Technology.* New York: Praeger Publishers. P. 23.
45. Hari Mohan Mathur. 1977. Introduction. *In* Hari Mohan Mathur (ed.). 1977. *Anthropology in the Development Process.* New Delhi: Vikas Publishing House Pvt Ltd. Also see, Richard B. Pollnac. 1981. *Socio-Cultural Aspects of Developing Small-Scale Fisheries: Delivering Services to the Poor.* Washington DC: The World Bank (Staff Working Paper No. 490).
46. Richard H. Brown. 1978. Towards a Communalist Approach to National Development Planning. *Public Administration Review,* Vol. 38, No. 3, May-June 1978, p. 265.
47. Martin C. Evans *et al.* 1979. *Sector Paper on Agriculture and Rural Development.* Manila: Asian Development Bank (A Bank Staff Working Paper). P. 17.
48. There is nothing new about distrust of the bureaucracy. See, John D. Montgomery. 1979. The Populist Front in Rural Development: Or Shall We Eliminate the Bureaucrats and Get on with the Job. *Public Administration Review,* Vol. 39, No. 1, January-February 1979.
49. Milton J. Easman. 1978. Development Administration and Constituency Organization. *Public Administration Review,* Vol. 38, No. 2, March-April 1978, p. 71.
50. See World Bank. 1983. *World Development Report 1983.* New York: Oxford University Press.
51. Peter T. Knight (ed.). 1980. *Implementing Programs of Human Development.* Washington DC: The World Bank (Staff Working Paper No. 403).
52. Samuel Paul. 1982. *Managing Development Programs.* Boulder, Colorado: Westview Press. P. 4.
53. Hari Mohan Mathur. 1982. The Role of Anthropologists in Rural Development. *IFDA Dossier,* 27, January-February 1982. Also see, Michael R. Dove. 1982. The Myth of the 'Communal' Longhouse in Rural Development: The Kantu of Kalimantan. *In* Colin MacAndrews and Chia Lin Sien (eds.). 1982. *Too Rapid Rural Development: Perceptions and Perspectives from Southeast Asia.* Athens, Ohio: Ohio University Press. Pp. 14-28.
54. John D. Montgomery. 1980. Administering to the Poor (Or, If We Can't Help Rich Dictators, What Can We Do for the Poor). *Public Administration Review,* Vol. 40, No. 5, September-October 1980, p. 423.

55. World Bank. 1978. *World Development Report 1978.* Washington DC: The World Bank.
56. FAO. 1982. Rural Poverty in Developing Countries and Means of Poverty Alleviation: World Review. *The State of Food and Agriculture 1981.* Rome: FAO of the UN. P. 107.
57. One form of agitation by government employees in India is resort to 'Work to Rule,' and this brings the business virtually to a halt. A sad commentary on the existing rules.
58. Alec McCallum. 1981. *Decentralization in Support of the Small Farmer.* Paper for the Inter-regional Seminar on Decentralization for Development organised by the UN DAD DTCD at Khartoum, 14-18 September 1981.
59. UNCRD. 1980. *Institutional Capability for Regional Development: Focus on Coordination.* Report of the Seminar held in Nagoya, Japan, 16-20 August 1980. Nagoya: United Nations Centre for Regional Development.
60. FAO. 1981. *Agriculture Toward 2000 AD.* Rome: FAO of the UN. Pp. 104-5.
61. Jerry VanSant. 1982. Managing Staff to Promote Participation. *RDPR* (Special Supplement on Integrated Rural Development), Vol. III, No. 3, Spring 1982, pp. 4-6. Also see, Gerald C. Papachiristou. 1980. The Indian Extension Staff: The Case for Revitalizing the Rural Bureaucracy. *Indian Journal of Public Administration*, 26 (2), April-June 1980, 303-19.
62. Richard Heaver. 1982. *Bureaucratic Politics and Incentives in the Management of Rural Development.* Washington DC: The World Bank (Staff Working Paper No. 537). P. 8.
63. David D. Gow and Jerry VanSant. 1981. *Beyond the Rhetoric of Rural Development Participation: How Can It Be Done?* Washington DC: Development Alternatives, Inc.
64. George Honadle and Philomene Makolo. 1982. Comparative Perspectives on Capacity Building for Development Administration. *Canadian Journal of Development Studies*, Spring Issue, 1982.
65. David C. Korten. 1980. Community Participation and Rural Development: A Learning Process Approach. *Public Administration Review*, Vol. 40, No. 5, September-October 1980, p. 484.
66. David C. Korten. 1980. Community Participation and Rural Development: A Learning Process Approach. *Public Administration Review*, Vol. 40, No. 5, September-October. p. 502.
67. Gunnar Myrdal and Dudley Seers. 1982. Where Has All the Aid Gone? *Express Magazine*, (*Indian Express*, Sunday Edition), 1 August 1982, p. 4. (By arrangement with *The Guardian*.)

Improving the Performance of Agricultural Development Administration

A dministering development programmes for small farmers has proved to be a much more complex task than was visualised earlier. World Development Report 1983 acknowledges this reality: 'Governments often find programmes involving the poorest are the most difficult to make effective.'[1] Partly, the reason is that here the administrators are on somewhat unfamiliar ground. There is not much previous experience to guide them in their operations. Concern for development of the poor is a relatively new phenomenon. Administrative methods appropriate for other general programmes for the community as a whole often fail to reach the poor as a separate target group.[2]

Emerging Developmental Challenges

It is important that improvements are seen quickly in the performance of small farmer agriculture development programmes. Many governments in the Third World, United Nations and other organisations concerned with international development are increasingly extending support to small farmer development both on grounds of equity to redress the imbalance which the earlier development efforts created and sheer expediency to see that small farmers, who contribute significantly to the total agricultural output in ways that are wholly economically viable, keep up their production levels.[3] But most emphatic in the expression of its support to small farmers was the World Conference on Agrarian Reform and Rural Development (WCARRD) organised by the Food and Agriculture Organization of the United Nations (FAO) in Rome in July 1979.

The conference adopted a Programme of Action focused on the poor and recommended a well thought out strategy for effective administration of agricultural services to meet their needs.[4]

Following this new concern for development of the small farmers, a number of development programmes have been launched in recent years. Targeted at the small farmers, these programmes seek to enhance their productivity, employment opportunities, incomes and participation in decision-making concerning local development. The rapidly increasing number of these programmes has not necessarily resulted in any significant change in the living standards of the rural poor. Rather the expansion has greatly strained the administrative capacity in most countries.[5] While there seems to be no way of avoiding these strains altogether, it should be possible to devise methods of easing them.

Some experience in equipping administration for its task of serving the small farmer is now available.[6] Five regional expert consultations, organised by the FAO since 1979, have generated not only a consensus on the need for administrative change but have also put forth a set of useful recommendations.[7] FAO can claim a share in the success achieved in bringing to the attention of policy-makers, administrators and scholars across the world the crucial importance of the administrative factor.[8] Agricultural development programmes, especially those designed to serve the small farmer, are highly sensitive to the quality of implementation. It would be true to say that 'the constraints on development are not technological or even financial but are essentially organizational and administrative.'[9]

In the past the failure to recognise the obvious fact that development programmes depend for their success on interactions at the boundary lines between field level administrators and small farmers has now given rise to numerous problems in implementation.[10] Public services specifically designed for small farmers often do not get across to them.[11] Frustrated with the way the government agencies operate, small farmers in many places now tend to steer away from them, preferring instead business as before with the village money-lender and other such traditional sources of support.

Adapting Administration to Small Farmer Needs

If success of the small farmer development programmes is dependent on the performance of agencies and staff at the field level, it is obvious that 'local action capabilities' be first strengthened. What improvements can help bring about this desired change? Before turning to a discussion on reforms in administration, it needs to be made clear that there can be no prescriptions which may be valid universally for all times. What may work in one situation may be quite unworkable in another. Therefore, full consideration needs to be given to the unique situation in each country before any reform measures are introduced in the administrative system.

To be effective the measures aimed at administrative reform need to have clearly defined objectives. A quick, perceptible improvement in the life style of small farmers should be stated as the goal for these measures from the very beginning. It was recently observed 'For a poverty-focused agriculture and rural development strategy the ultimate criterion must be the impact of governmental performance on the ground, rather than at other levels or on the 'modernization' of governmental procedures as objectives in themselves.'[12]

Further, the task of reform will be greatly facilitated if it is borne in mind that the requirements of administering small farmer development programmes are in many ways quite distinctive. Some of the special features and problems concerned with poverty-focused agricultural development include the following:

1. The programmes seek to bring about changes from a traditional pattern of production services (for example, credit from the bank instead of from the money-lender).
2. The multitude of small farmers scattered in the countryside must be involved in the decision-making process if the extension agent is to stimulate behavioural change that might favour acceptance of new ideas.
3. Government officials and the rural poor are separated by differences in their social background, education and other factors, and this does come in the way of bringing the two together.
4. In the field government functionaries are under increasing pressure both from above and below (the local elites) to favour the affluent in the countryside.
5. Many of the programmes which percolate down to the village level require considerable modification to be useful locally; however, the rigidity of procedures does not allow local functionaries to make the necessary changes on their own.
6. Powers of the field administrators are extremely limited. They must always look to above for orders.
7. Cumbersome rules and procedures are a hindrance to quick

action or to meet the requirements of specific situations.

8. Agricultural services are not all the responsibility of any one line agency. The multiplicity of agencies, each delivering its own particular service or input, creates problems for their delivery to the farmers in a coordinated manner.

9. Often the developmental goals may be abstract (for example, community self-reliance). It is not possible to measure the achievement of such targets.

Creating organisational structures, designing administrative procedures, and developing managerial skills to cope with the demands of small farmer programmes present an unusual challenge.[13] Public administration has not yet acquired a fully developmental orientation. Consequently, the conduct of development operations continues to be hindered by such characteristic features of bureaucracy as over-centralisation, proliferation of units and staff, absence of effective coordination, endless inter-departmental rivalries and conflicts, lack of accountability, little or no incentives, slow decision-making processes, rigidity of rules, preference for status quo, etc.[14] Moreover, the development task is not helped by the field staff which is not only insufficient in number, but also indifferently trained, inadequately equipped, poorly paid and ill-motivated. There are many who genuinely believe that bureaucratic action by itself is incapable of achieving development for the rural poor.

Indeed, this task of rendering service to the small farmers can also be entrusted to non-governmental organisations (NGOs) and many other forms of institutional arrangements. In India, agricultural services were being provided through democratically elected bodies at the block level (Panchayat Samitis) during the early 1960s, but a decade later in the early 1970s these functions were transferred to other governmental agencies specially created for the purpose. Surely, as one observer put it 'At present there is no realistic alternative to the use of government services....'[15] Thus, the task has everywhere fallen on the governmental agencies in the districts, blocks and villages — at administrative levels closest to the small farmer.

Measures for improvement in the existing administrative system to serve the small farmer can be designed and put into operation provided the objectives of the development programmes and the specific requirements for their implementation are constantly kept in view. It is not possible here to consider in detail the many adaptations in administration which will be necessary for making agricultural services accessible to a wide segment of poor·farmers. But it seems necessary to emphasise the need for decentralisation of powers and functions from higher levels in the administration to the field level, effective coordination among agencies at all levels, free communication among various hierarchical levels and better information and monitoring systems:[16]

1. Decentralisation can work only if it has high-level backing. While bureaucrats may be willing to give up certain functions, they are not always so willing to give up their powers. Moreover, rural development is not a task which highly centralised and stratified bureaucracies can accomplish without the involvement of field staff.

2. Coordination problems can often be minimised by simplifying the programmes through a reduction in the number of components. The success of many low income people-centred programmes is due to the fact that they were designed with just one purpose in mind: for example, population planning in Indonesia, T and V system in India, tea development in Kenya, rural education in Mexico. In some countries the chief administrative officer in the districts has been able to achieve effective coordination because of the prestige which he has traditionally enjoyed. But his workload on this account is becoming very heavy. Also, resentment among technical personnel is growing about his style of functioning. Committees have been set up in other places to achieve effective coordination. Whatever ensures that 'the cylinders fire' in the right order, at the right time, must be allowed to continue.[17] But it is important that coordinating agencies are clothed with sufficient status and authority.

3. A monitoring system can serve to maintain control over the field staff without undue interference in their sphere of delegated routine and day-to-day working, and can help to motivate them to perform better. But it is essential to develop the system in a way that, while all the required information becomes available to the top levels, the field level staff is not diverted from implementing programmes merely to be able to operate an elaborate reporting system for its own sake.

In operating the delivery system the field level officials tend to bypass the local organisations. Delivery services will improve considerably if an effort is made to win local organisations on the side of the governmental agencies.[18] It is impossible for the field staff to 'conduct a dialogue with millions of individual farmers.'[19] They can be reached far more easily through their own organisations. In fact, governmental agencies should help small farmers to form their own organisations. This will make easier the task of delivering services and will stimulate the involvement of people in the development process. The existence of such participatory organisations will also create external pressures on the governmental agencies to be more responsive and better managed.

Commitment of Field Staff to Poverty-Focused Programmes

Improvement in the organisation of governmental business by itself will not produce a very significant change in the performance of agricultural services meant for small farmers.[20] A lot will depend on the field administrators — their social background, education, training, commitment to rural development, motivation, to name some of the factors that affect the level of performance. The personnel factors in improving administration of development programmes for small farmers have not yet received full attention.[21] As a result the administration of these programmes is now in the hands of those who are least able to cope with its complexities.

It is not only a question of staff shortages, though the importance of that factor is undeniable. The number of farmers which a village level official is required to serve is extremely large.[22] He has no transport to tour within his jurisdiction. It is not surprising, therefore, that he prefers to visit roadside villages which are conveniently connected by public transport. Often he stays in some town away from the villages in his charge both because he cannot find accommodation there and also because he prefers to stay with his family in the town which certainly offers better living conditions.

Training which the field administrators receive at the beginning of their career is of an indifferent quality. Many of them do not know their job well enough. Often farmers know more about agriculture than the agricultural extension agents in the initial years of their service. Consequently, their ignorance produces an effect just the opposite of what the field organisations are intended to achieve. Salaries paid to the field level officials continue to be amongst the lowest anywhere. 'As a result the more promising and competent field workers are lost to other preoccupations.'[23] The arduous nature of their work is not given sufficient recognition. The supervisory officers on inspection visits find nothing commendable to report on the field staff. Only blame for failures is highlighted in their performance appraisal, even when the failures may not be due to their actions alone.

Sooner rather than later, many field administrators lose zest for their work. This further affects the already poor performance of agricultural services. They continue to work, but without any motivation. The small farmer who is the object of all development endeavours does not matter much to officials who lack commitment. There is no place for the beneficiaries — the small farmers — in their world of work.

The service to small farmers which has remained a weak link in many agricultural development projects will improve only when concerted action is taken to bring about the required 'bureaucratic re-orientation' at the operational levels.[24] Here motivation makes a very significant difference to the performance level. Emphasising the importance of this factor Richard Heaver says: 'Real commitment to project goals can produce results despite ill-conceived structures and untrained manpower, while poorly motivated managers will achieve little with the best of training and in the most appropriate of structures.'[25] The commitment of field personnel to serve the poor in rural areas will increase if sufficient attention is paid to the following factors which have a direct bearing on the job performance:

1. *Methods of Recruitment:* In most countries the educational level and results of recruitment examinations constitute the basis for selection to field staff positions. There are no tests to determine the aptitude for work in a rural setting. Usually the successful candidates come from an urban background. Often agricultural development officials are men even in societies where farming operations are done mostly by women. Obviously there is a need to change the selection methods so that those joining the development cadres have the appropriate

qualifications and the right attitude to serving the small farmers.

2. *Training*: At the entry point in service the field officials undergo some training. But this training does not equip them adequately. It concentrates on purely technical aspects of their work. It does not teach them about the dynamics of rural society and the ways of working with small farmers and their organisations. There are no opportunities later during their career to brush up even their technical knowledge, and as a result they are soon out of touch with the newer developments. The T and V System of Extension is an attempt to keep the staff up-to-date with the latest technical information and communication skills.[26] But much more needs to be done.

3. *Compensation*:In relation to the difficult conditions of work the salary levels are very low. Unless something is done to improve this situation, it will be difficult to recruit competent persons.

4. *Job Descriptions*:It is now being appreciated that rather than having a multi-purpose worker it will be better to have field level officials who devote their attention full-time to agricultural work. But even where such positions exist, other government functions (such as elections, national savings, family planning) continue to divert them from their main task. Hence the need to define the jobs. But job descriptions must be precise and realistic so that the field officials know what exactly is expected of them.

5. *Performance Appraisal* In the absence of clear job definitions the performance is appraised not on the basis of any objective criterion but on purely subjective considerations. This is not a fair system. It does not motivate the staff to do its best. It is important to develop objective criteria to judge the performance of field staff in serving the needs of small farmers.

6. *Responsibility and Authority*:Field level staff find that they cannot carry out fully their responsibilities in the field simply because they lack sufficient authority. There is a need for delegation of more authority to lower levels commensurate with their responsibility.

. *Promotion and Career Development* Under the existing personnel systems it is difficult for field level officials to move up the hierarchical ladder. Higher level posts are reserved for members of certain cadres. To keep the field staff at the same low level for years is to condemn them to dead-end jobs which can seriously impair their morale and job performance. There should be some rewards for satisfactory performance either in the shape of promotion to higher positions or salary increases at various stages in the career.

In addition to the above, it is necessary to instil in the field staff a feeling that their role is important. This can be done by their increased involvement in various tasks connected with planning and administration. Things will move fast only when the lower level functionaries think that they are getting a fair deal from the higher echelons. The following observations are very apt in this context:

> People tend to deal with others as they have been dealt with themselves. An agricultural extension agent who must function according to typically rigid bureaucratic procedures, rules and precedents is unlikely to approach farmers with flexibility and responsiveness needed to encourage meaningful response to project initiatives. On the other hand, an agent who has been actively involved in decisions related to his or her own activities, is more likely to serve farmers in a manner that appreciates and respects their potential to contribute to project decisions affecting them.[27]

Training for Better Administrative Performance

Training, especially for administrators of agricultural development programmes, does not seem to have received sufficient attention in the earlier development efforts. Compared to institutions providing training for personnel from other development sectors, the number of existing institutions to train agricultural administrators is rather insignificant. This lack of adequate management training for agricultural administrators was recently observed:

> Traditionally, very little is done to provide training for those who administer agricultural development programmes in developing countries. For the main cadre of administrators who administer

programmes of central government at national, provincial and district levels there is little, if any, attention given in training programmes to the increasing complexity of the agricultural development process and the role which governments play in its promotion. For the technocrats in ministries concerned with agriculture the emphasis of training generally has a strong technical orientation.[28]

The scarcity of trained manpower to cope with the new challenges in small farmer agricultural development is thus attributable, in a considerable measure, to the persistence of indifference towards training. Knowledge, skills and attitudes needed to plan and administer development programmes for the small farmer are of a kind different from other programmes that have existed all these years. Successful implementation of these programmes depends on the availability of administrators who (*a*) have a clear perception of the issues involved in the development process; (*b*) possess the requisite administrative/managerial skills; and (*c*) are imbued with a spirit of service to the poor.

However, it is quite possible to build up the requisite administrative strength through a well planned training intervention.[29] Indeed, developments which have occurred in the field of training in recent years are very promising and, therefore, have encouraged the belief that training can 'help organizations be more effective in the delivery of goods and services'.[30] Believing that training is part of the answer to issues connected with improving the performance of organisations created to serve the small farmers, WCARRD in its Programme of Action enjoined upon the governments, FAO and others concerned to institute training programmes for policy-makers and administrators 'specially to improve their understanding of the condition and problems of rural areas and their ability to respond to the needs of the rural poor.'[31]

However, training can help produce administrators of the kind and in numbers required only if it is conducted in a proper manner. Traditional approaches to training have failed to produce the intended impact.[32] Any training strategy which hopes to help improve the administration of programmes for small farmer development should give full consideration to the following propositions:

1. It is important to keep in view the special features of agriculture

and rural development which determine the nature of administrative tasks for accomplishing the developmental goals. However important, the standard management training courses will not help develop the knowledge, skills and attitudes which field administrators must possess to be effective in their work.

2. Training as a discreet event conducted in isolation from and without adequate support of the development organisations whom it is meant to serve will be of little help. It must be regarded as one element in an overall plan of administrative reform. By bringing administrators from various levels and backgrounds together training must provide them with an opportunity not only to learn about management matters but also to examine objectives and priorities of the programmes with a view to redefining them if necessary.

3. Such job relevant training must necessarily be 'in-service'. As job requirements change due to rapid changes all around, training cannot be confined to only one point in the career. It has to be a continuous process of learning from experience, and learning to implement the newly acquired knowledge in the field.

4. While some outside assistance may be helpful, the training programme is best organised nationally. As problems of the rural poor are situation specific, it is nationally organised training which alone can respond to the training needs of the development personnel in any country.

Once the above propositions are accepted, the planning of training to improve the organisation and administration of agricultural services for small farmers can be done in a systematic manner. This planning exercise would involve several major steps:

1. A training unit must first be established. The Ministry of Agriculture would appear to be the best location for purely practical considerations. This must be headed by a senior official preferably with some background in training.[33]

2. A detailed plan document must be prepared. The plan should clearly lay down the nature of training needed by functionaries at different levels, the number of people to be trained, the resources needed for the purpose, etc.

3. Many training programmes do not seem to be serving their clientele well enough chiefly because they are not based on a carefully conducted survey of training needs. It is necessary to determine the exact training needs of all functionaries at various levels.
4. The curricula should include subjects relevant to the needs of small farmer development. Besides a knowledge of socio-economic conditions, the emphasis should be on orienting the staff towards serving the small farmer.
5. In in-service training the lecture method should have a limited role. More participatory methods must be brought into use. Classroom based instruction alone will not be enough. Some exposure to problems in the field seems necessary. Seminars will elicit better response from the higher level officials. A number of new training approaches have currently come into use including (*a*) action learning; (*b*) integrated training programmes; (*c*) performance improvement planning (PIP); and (*d*) modular training. These have all been designed to improve the relevance of training to the job needs. Elements from these approaches can be profitably utilised in organising training to improve the overall performance of small farmer development programmes.
6. To be effective training must be provided to officials at all levels, including the highest, and there must be provision for providing this in-service training whenever it becomes so necessary in view of the emerging developmental challenges.
7. The success of this training plan will depend on the quality of trainers, and presently trainers are in short supply everywhere. The issue of first training the trainers themselves is, therefore, extremely urgent.[34] FAO has initiated some action in this direction.

Improvements in training are thus expected to further reinforce the other efforts currently being made to produce in the field a direct impact on the performance of agricultural services for small farmers.

NOTES AND REFERENCES

1. World Bank. 1983. *World Development Report, 1983.* Washington DC: Oxford University Press. P. 88.
2. SFDT. 1978. *Small Farmer Development Manual.* Volume I: *Field Action for Small Farmers, Small Fishermen and Peasants.* Bangkok: Regional Office for Asia and the Far East, FAO of the UN. Table 1, p. 4 gives examples of distinctions between programme priorities for the whole community and those for small farmers.
3. World Bank. 1975. *Rural Development: Sector Paper.* Washington DC: The World Bank.
4. FAO. 1981. *The Declaration of Principles and Programme of Action of the World Conference on Agrarian Reform and Rural Development.* Rome: FAO of the UN.
5. Martin C. Evans *et al.* 1979. *Sector Paper on Agriculture and Rural Development.* Manila: Asian Development Bank (A Bank Staff Working Paper). P. 16.
6. A.T. Mosher. 1981. *Three Ways to Spur Agricultural Growth.* New York: International Agricultural Development Service. See Part 3: Improving the Efficiency of Regular Agricultural Services.
7. Asia and Pacific, Manila (1979), Near East, Nicosia (1980), Latin America and Caribbean, Mexico (1981), Africa, English-speaking, Nairobi (1982), and Africa, French-speaking, Douala (1983).
8. This year the World Bank had chosen the theme 'Management in Development' for its *World Development Report, 1983* to highlight the important role which the administration plays in the development process.
9. Alec McCallum. 1980. Unsnarling the Bureaucracy: Devolution and Rural Development. *CERES,* Vol. 13, No. 2, March-April 1980, p. 36.
10. Byron T. Mook. 1982. *The World of the Indian Field Administrator.* New Delhi: Vikas Publishing House Pvt Ltd.
11. Hari Mohan Mathur. 1983. *Reaching the Poor in Rural Areas: Developmental Issues and Administrative Requirements.* Kuala Lumpur: United Nations Asian and Pacific Development Centre.
12. S. Ramakrishnan and A. McCallum. 1982. The Role of Training in Improving the Organization and Administration of Agricultural Services to Small Farmers. *In* FAO. 1982. *Improving the Organization and Administration of Agricultural Services for Small Farmers in Africa.* Report of a Regional Expert Consultation held in Nairobi, Kenya, December 1982. Rome: FAO of the UN. P. 66.
13. FAO. 1981. *Administering Agricultural Development for Small Farmers.* (FAO Economic and Social Development Paper 20). Rome: FAO of the UN.
14. Alec McCallum. 1981. Why Improve the Organization and Administration of Agricultural Development in the Near East. Report of a Regional Expert Consultation held in Nicosia, Cyprus, December 1980. Rome: FAO of the UN.
15. Guy Hunter. 1982. *Enlisting the Small Farmer: The Range of Requirements.* London: Overseas Development Institute. P. 39.
16. Hari Mohan Mathur. 1981. *Administrative Capability for Rural Development.*

Paris: Institute International d'Administration Publique. (Lecture delivered on 22 December 1981).

17. FAO. 1981. *Delivery Systems in Support of the Small Farmer in Asia.* Rome: FAO of the UN. P. 46.

18. Michael M. Cernea. 1981. Modernization and Development Potential of Traditional Grass-Roots Peasant Organizations. *In* Mustafa O. Attir *et al.* (eds.). 1981. *Directions of Change: Modernization Theory, Research and Realities.* Boulder, Colorado: Westview Press.

19. M. P. Cracknell and J. H. Feingold. 1982. Including the Marginal Producer. *CERES,* May-June 1982, p. 16.

20. Milton J. Easman. 1983. *Paraprofessionals in Rural Development: Issues in Field-Level Staffing for Agricultural Projects.* Washington DC: The World Bank (Staff Working Paper No. 573).

21. Robert W. Iversen. 1979. Personnel for Implementation: A Contextual Perspective. *In* George Honadle and Rudi Klauss (eds.). 1981. *International Development Administration.* New York: Praeger. Pp. 87-98.

22. S. Ramakrishnan. 1982. Issues on the Organization and Administration of Agricultural Services for Small Farmers in Africa. *In* FAO. 1982. *Improving the Organization and Administration of Agricultural Services for Small Farmers in Africa.* Report of a Regional Expert Consultation held in Nairobi, Kenya, December 1982. Rome: FAO of the UN. P. 38 of this paper gives some data on the ratio of extension workers to farmers from three African countries.

23. Hiroshi Yokota. 1983. *Agricultural Administration at the Village Level in Asia.* Tokyo: Asian Productivity Organization. P. 8.

24. David Korten and Norman Uphoff. 1981. *Bureaucratic Reorientation for Participatory Development.* (NASPAA Working Paper 1). Washington DC: National Association of Schools of Public Affairs and Administration.

25. Richard Heaver. 1982. *Bureaucratic Politics and Incentives in the Management of Rural Development.* Washington DC: The World Bank (Staff Working Paper No. 537). P. 8.

26. Daniel Benor and James Q. Harrison. 1977. *Agricultural Extension: The Training and Visit System.* Washington DC: The World Bank.

27. Jerry VanSant, David Gow and Thomas Armor. 1982. Managing Staff to Promote Participation. *RDPR* (Special Supplement on Integrated Rural Development), Vol. III, No. 2, Spring 1982, p. 4.

28. S. Ramakrishnan and Alec McCallum. 1982. The Role of Training in Improving the Organization and Administration of Agricultural Services to Small Farmers. *Improving the Organization and Administration of Agricultural Services for Small Farmers in Africa.* Report of a Regional Expert Consultation held in Nairobi, Kenya, December 1982. Rome: FAO of the UN. P. 64.

29. Hari Mohan Mathur. 1983. *Training of Development Administrators.* Kuala Lumpur: United Nations Asian and Pacific Development Centre.

30. UN. 1976. *The Role of Training of Trainers in Administrative Development.* A Working Paper prepared in the Division of Public Administration and Finance, United Nations, for Inter-regional Workshop on the Training of Trainers, Vienna, July 1976.

31. FAO. 1979. *World Conference on Agrarian Reform and Rural Development Report.* Rome: FAO of the UN. P. 15.

32. George Honadle and John P. Hannah. 1982. Management Performance for Rural Development. Packaged Training or Capacity Building. *Public Administration and Development,* Vol. 2, 295-307.
33. Hari Mohan Mathur. 1980. Organization and Establishment of a Nationally Organized Training Programme. *Improving the Organization and Administration of Agricultural Development in the Near East.* Report of an Expert Consultation held in Nicosia, Cyprus, December 1980. Rome: FAO of the UN. Pp. 34-41.
34. FAO. 1979. *Improving the Organization and Administration of Agricultural Development.* Report of an Expert Consultation held in Manila, Philippines, September 1979. Rome: FAO of the UN.

Development, Administrative Capability and Training

In most Third World countries nationally as well as internationally organised efforts to promote rapid socio-economic development do not yet seem to be producing the intended impact.[1] Further, it is becoming increasingly evident that the inability of development to yield the promised results is largely attributable to the weaknesses in administration.[2] Quite naturally, the disappointing results of government-administered development programmes are at present a source of great concern to all those engaged in furthering the development process.[3]

During the past three decades, governments and international donors allocated considerable resources to the task of stimulating development in the Third World. In some cases this effort led to remarkable achievements, but reports now coming in from many others places highlight the enormous difficulties encountered in implementing the development projects.[4] Public services specifically designed for the poor largely remain well beyond their reach.[5] Even where permitted, participation of the target groups in the development process has still to emerge as a potent force.[6] The reported cases of successful development continue to be few and far between. Rather, it is the haltingly moving programmes and projects which all these years have dominated the development scene.[7]

Administrative Issues in the Third World

Evidence is rapidly mounting in support of the view that the poor performance of most programmes and projects is due to their poor management.[8] Often farmers are unable to get seeds, fertilisers and other inputs on time, not because supplies are inadequate but, because the development organisations especially those at the field level are not fully equipped for the task. Recent World Bank experience confirms that management problems constitute the main obstacle to successful implementation of its development projects. And in recognition of the significance of the administrative factor the World Development Report 1983 is focused on the management of development programmes.[9]

Comments by Edward A Kieloch on administrative shortcomings in India's Intensive Agricultural Development Programme (IADP) of the early 1960s would still be applicable to the present-day situation in many places:

> All too often the promised fertilisers and improved seeds do not arrive in time for planting. Not infrequently, the farmers are unable to get a loan in time to purchase package inputs simply because of inefficiencies and delays in processing loan applications. Demonstration equipment lies idle for lack of repair and soil testing falls months behind schedule. Crop spoilage occurs for lack of storage, processing or transportation facilities and various kinds of technical information which should have been conveyed to the farmers were not, often with dire consequences. In sum, agricultural development is being depressed by administrative ineffectiveness.[10]

In Africa, development has continued to lag behind mainly because of administrative inadequacies. It was recently noted:

> The symptoms of an inadequately staffed public administration showed up in the form of reduced capacity to implement policies (especially those which required a high degree of coordination) and low standards of maintenance and operating efficiency in running public facilities like rural water supply systems, roads and health facilities, leading in many cases to premature destruction of expensive capital assets.[11]

Indeed, ineffective administration is now increasingly recognised as an endemic source of trouble for a large number of development programmes.

The desire to accelerate the pace of development has further complicated matters.[12] Almost everywhere numerous organisations and agencies have sprung up to implement the development plans. Alec McCallum pointed out that this proliferation of newly created units to administer development programmes has only produced some well known negative side effects, including wasteful duplication of functions, insurmountable problems of coordination, endless inter-agency rivalries and conflicts.[13] In many cases persons lacking even basic managerial skills have been saddled with responsibilities for development in very senior administrative positions. It is clear that such development organisations cannot cope with the demands made on them for the provision of administrative skills of the kind needed to plan and implement the highly complex development projects. On the basis of his Ghanian experience, Berg concluded:

> A large increase in the size and character of the tasks imposed on a weak administrative system does not simply mean that the capacity to perform declines marginally. Rather it tends to set into motion forces that erode the whole decision-making machinery and destroy the capacity to execute and control.[14]

Investments in development projects which have sharply increased in recent years have not led to any improvement in the situation either.[15] Often funds meant for various development schemes remain unutilised simply because the administration with its existing resources is not in a position to undertake all the needed action within the time available. In connection with the development of tribal areas in India, an expert group made these observations:

> For the first time since independence, massive ... financial inputs have been made available in these areas. While these investments have been rising, a corresponding matching administrative framework has not been brought into existence ... with the result that outlays ... have not been utilized fully. Thus the objective of benefits accruing to the tribals has been incompletely realized.[16]

Other experiences also suggest that the traditional administrative system cannot adequately handle the new development tasks.

This inadequacy of the administration to respond to newly emerging development challenges has largely to do with the fact that earlier development efforts failed to appreciate the true significance of administrative capability as a key factor in the overall development process, and, therefore, took no concrete steps to promote administrative development. A UN document noted:

Administrative capability — though a key determinant in the success or failure of a plan — has not been one of the main preoccupations of development planners. It has been taken for granted as a constant. It has normally been assumed that the capability of the on-going system is sufficient to carry out the more complex tasks demanded by increasingly sophisticated development plans. The administrative feasibility of projects, where it has been looked into has been confined to such matters as increased personnel requirements, rather than the more fundamental issues of administrative capability. Even where administrative reform efforts have been launched, they have generally been attempted in isolation without being directly related to the needs of national development plans.[17]

In the same vein another UN document adds:

Although the importance of public administration for national development has been frequently stressed by national and international entities, the measures taken and resources made available to effect improvements have seldom been commensurate with what was needed and possible.... The erroneous notion persists that the cost of administration and even of administrative improvement is intrinsically unproductive and wasteful.[18]

Under such conditions it was not unusual to launch development plans without first ascertaining whether the administrative machinery had the requisite strength to implement them. The capability of administration to implement development plans was just taken for granted. No effort was made to visualise the problems that could arise later and upset the entire process of implementation. Planners only hoped that everything would turn out fine and that their plans would eventually contribute to the well being of the poor.

However, this situation is now rapidly changing. The contribution of public management to national development is beginning to be recognised more readily than before.[19] Emphasising the critical importance of the management factor, Sridath Ramphal even went to the extent of declaring that development was all management.[20] Most planners today will have no difficulty in agreeing with what Toulmin and Chandradhat observed some years ago:

> Good public management... is vital to development. If other prerequisites are present to a sufficient degree, and if public management is generally good, then there will be developmental progress. If, however, other prerequisites are present but public management is poor, there will be less progress and perhaps none at all.[21]

In current development literature an observation that appears time and again is that 'the constraints on development are not technological or even financial but are essentially organizational and administrative.'[22] Arguing that management was an even more important factor than either capital or technology, Anthony Bottrall emphatically concluded:

> There is an increasingly large and convincing body of evidence accumulating which points to major deficiencies of management on many irrigation schemes in ldcs. There are, therefore, good grounds for arguing that very substantial benefits could be achieved by a concentration of effort on improving management and institutions, without immediate recourse to much of the capital investment in improved technology which many have hitherto believed necessary. To bring about these improvements, action is needed on ... measures to strengthen the management capabilities of official staff.[23]

Jedlicka has also made a point concerning this issue: 'One of the increasing realities of solving the problems of the developing countries is that perhaps even more important than the physical-resource limitation these countries face, the organizational limitations — the sheer inability to adopt appropriate management styles of behaviour that can get the job done — may be even more overwhelming.'[24]

Recognising the vital role of administration in development, a recent Asian Development Bank document noted: 'Substantial inputs of intangible but essential factors such as administrative skill, managerial leadership and entrepreneurial flair will be required if the plans on paper are to be translated into successful projects on the ground.[25] But at the same time this document lamented: 'Skills and knowledge for planning and management are rapidly becoming some of the scarcest resources in the DMCs. There are signs in some cases that the ability to implement projects efficiently is falling behind the governments' capacity to finance them.[26]

What should these countries lacking administrative capability of the required kind do in the circumstances? Should the scale of existing development operations be reduced to bring it in line with the administrative capability presently available? There seems no chance for such a suggestion getting acceptance anywhere. The Third World countries are nations in a hurry. Planners in these countries are committed to policies designed to secure speedily a better way of life for masses of their people, most of whom have always lived in abject poverty. And the poor are now unwilling to wait any further. For these countries socio-economic progress at an accelerated pace would be the most desirable development objective to pursue.[27]

The use of foreign experts is sometimes recommended as a way of overcoming the manpower shortages, a variety of which exists in most developing countries. Unquestionably, foreign experts can make a significant contribution to the promotion of development at a fast pace. However, several difficulties in their long and extensive use on various development projects have lately been experienced. One point of criticism is that a heavy dependence on experts from abroad is likely to further aggravate the problem of lack of managerial expertise that afflicts many governments. In any case, this cannot be regarded as a satisfactory long-term solution to the problem of matching administration to the newly emerging developmental challenges.

It appears that there is only one way in which Third World countries aspiring to higher levels of living can proceed to realise their development goals. They must initiate action urgently to build up the managerial competence.[28] As Pierre Vinde recently pointed out, it is extremely important for the developing countries themselves to have sufficient administrative capability.[29] The developing countries' ability to formulate policies, to plan, to manage and to review their operations is becoming more and more essential. Such efforts should be continued in order to remedy the shortcomings of public management, whose soundness is a priority for development.

A considerable increase in administrative capability will be required to translate the development plans into effective programmes of action. [30] The success or failure of development depends on the ability of development organisations to identify and define problems, formulate policies and programmes of development, determine priorities among competing demands, allocate resources, develop manpower, use science and technology for development, and implement development plans and projects.[31]

Development and Development Administration

The word 'development' is often bandied around as if there were a general consensus on what it means. In actual fact, the central issues in development have provoked some bitter controversies: Development for what purpose? Development towards what end?[32] There is unanimity on the point that development must lead to the eradication of absolute poverty. However, on many other issues the debate is marked by sharp conflicts of opinion.

In the minds of most people, especially in the West, development is equivalent to modernisation which is believed to represent the triumph of Western materialism. It means moving towards 'a society of skyscrapers, with televisions in every home, cars in every garage and combine harvesters in the fields, with everyone working in humming factories and carpeted offices.'[33] To these people development only means an endless pursuit of growth. Where it would all lead to does not bother them at all.

Possibly the benefits of this kind of development will eventually trickle down. But there is no definite indication of time. And the perspectives of the planners and the poor on time are quite different. A ten - or a five - year time - frame may not appear to be too long to the planner working in the comfort of his office in the national capital, but the poor, landless agricultural worker struggling in the distant village to find some employment during the slack season cannot be expected to wait patiently for the benefits from development to reach him some day eventually.[34]

This model of development is also likely to destroy the values which traditional societies have cherished through the ages. It is these values which have enabled the traditional societies to face many crises. The family life, the village life are now undergoing a process of rapid transformation. The traditions which bound people together in work, in worship and in other enterprises, and the values which fostered egalitarianism are all dying at a rapid pace. Indeed, the very bases of traditional society are cracking up against the onslaught of modernising forces.[35]

Some thinkers are now talking of 'another development'. While seeking to remove the curse of want, this model of development will strive for the retention and propagation of the original values of societies in the Third World. Surely, the objective of development cannot be to just expand the material wealth; it must emphasise the development of all men and women to their full potential.[36] With all its riches, the West is really in no position to provide an example of development to the Third World where even the undernourished people still live by the pristine socio-cultural values which technologically advanced societies are tending to discard rapidly. Their development goals will need to be defined by the developing countries themselves. Increasingly, it is now being realised that:

There is no model of development that can achieve all the development objectives simultaneously and in all countries. In the face of so much diversity among people, countries, and regions, we have to give up the effort to find a single definition of development or to discover a universally applicable theory or strategy of development. We should accept the necessity of a range of development strategies.[37]

The development task facing administrators in the Third World is an enormously complicated one.[38] Here, the administrator is expected to allocate the scarce resources for development among sectors that all claim the highest priority, to increase foreign exchange earnings through export to markets that are all but closed to the free flow of goods and services, to feed the rapidly growing populations in the face of persisting difficulties on the agricultural front, to deliver inputs and services for development to the very poor in distant rural areas who do not seem very enthusiastic to participate in development programmes specially designed for them.

The paternalistic style of functioning is no longer workable. It was

recently observed that 'The manager of public development programmes is expected to be highly sensitive to the needs of the people
and, therefore, capable of gearing his operations to provide for an
effective, efficient and equitable delivery system especially where
the needs of the people are concerned.'[39] To be effective, the
administrator must learn to work with the people and stimulate
changes in societies that have for long remained stagnant.

As development problems become complex, the role of public
administration becomes even more important. Indeed, the administrative capability will henceforth be a crucial factor in the development process. A UN document recently noted that 'Administrative
capacity is a major and crucial factor in the success or failure of
development efforts.'[40] To overcome administrative inadequacies,
governments in the developing countries need seriously to adopt
appropriate steps to improve their administrative systems. Small
measures, adopted haltingly, will suffice no more. It will not be possible to make discernible progress without devoting to this task the
attention it deserves. A successful response to the development
challenge calls for a genuine commitment to administrative
development and must include a variety of concrete measures to
promote it. Nothing short of such a dynamic approach can hope to
succeed in realising all the development objectives.

In this context, a recent resolution of the Economic and Social
Council of the United Nations is of very special significance. This
resolution calls upon 'the Specialised Agencies to recognize that
increased administrative capability for developing countries is indispensable for meeting their needs in the 1980s, requiring action at
national and international levels to create such capability.'[41] Echo-
ing this concern, a group of development administration experts at
a UN meeting urged that 'the international development strategy
for the Third United Nations Development Decade should draw the
attention of developing countries to the urgency of enhancing their
institutional and managerial capabilities to meet the challenges of
development in the 1980s and beyond.'[42]

The Significance of Trained Manpower

In an effort to strengthen the implementation capability of their
administrative systems, Third World countries have taken several

new initiatives in recent years. Training to prepare the government officials for their enlarged role as development administrators has received considerable attention everywhere.[43] This interest in training arises from the realisation that lack of trained manpower poses obstacles to development as formidable as those pertaining to scarce resources, inadequate capital and insufficient technology.[44] Surely what development needs most of all is trained manpower. As Dag Hammerskjold once remarked:

> Great economic development programmes have been planned which were held back more by lack of men to direct them than by lack of capital. Great national problems of social welfare are failing to move forward primarily for lack of experienced officials to undertake the manifold administrative tasks which they entail. Fundamentally, man is the key to all problems, not money. Funds are valuable only when used by trained, experienced, and devoted men and women. Such people, on the other hand, can work miracles even with small resources and draw wealth out of a barren land.[45]

The World Bank recently reported that 'Shortage of trained manpower is a serious obstacle to the large-scale development of rural areas.'[46] Indeed, a cadre of trained personnel is as important to developing countries as other inputs like finance, machinery, etc. Emphasising the importance of training, the World Development Report 1980 states: 'Funds, equipment and advanced technologies can seldom substitute for trained field personnel or administrators.'[47]

Increasingly, it is being recognised that government officials have a key role to a play in promoting development, and that training can make them more effective as planners and administrators of development programmes. Irving Swerdlow and Marcus Ingle observed:

> No imaginative statistician has succeeded in developing unambiguous quantitative measurements that relate administrative capabilities to the scope, duration, and subject content of training programmes. Yet all over the world there appears to be a firm conviction that training government administrators is one of the ways of improving the operating efficiency of government agencies.[48]

A brochure containing information on the Government of India's Training Division notes:

> Success in this development endeavour is wholly dependent on the way the administrators perform their new development-oriented job. The problems which administrators currently face cannot be handled effectively by the traditional ways of doing government business. It is, therefore, important that the public administration system acquires a growing sophistication of administrative capabilities. A widespread belief now is that training can considerably help in making administration an instrument for accomplishing the tasks it has set for itself.[49]

On the role of training, it was recently observed at an FAO Expert Consultation that 'Relevant experience of some countries indicated that training created the opportunities not only for improved individual performance but also had great potential for organizational development.'[50] Further highlighting the belief in the value of training is the observation that 'Inadequate administration has long been recognized as a major constraint in achieving satisfactory rates of economic and social development. While it would be naive to claim that this inadequacy can be completely solved by training, certainly more and better quality training must be part of the complex answer.'[51]

Generally convinced that the surest method to improve administration for development is through training, development experts have for some time been arguing the case for more and more training. The advice to governments in the developing countries for establishing training institutes and organising training programmes has come from several quarters, including the United Nations agencies.[52] Commending training, Milton Easman urged that 'Invest heavily in the continuing education and training of public administrators, both generalists and programme specialists and at all levels of service.... Administrators should be brought into training situations frequently.'[53]

As a means of easing constraints to development caused by a lack of trained manpower and, thereby, improving the overall administrative capability for development, training has witnessed a phenomenal growth in recent years. The number of institutes engaged in development-oriented training, the number of training programmes and the number of participants have rapidly increased.[54] A major impetus for the expansion of training has come from international donors.

The World Bank, the international organisation most concerned with development, took early initiatives to start training on a systematic basis. In 1951 it sponsored in cooperation with the Economic Commission for Latin America (ECLA) a seminar on the preparation of development projects. 'After this first experiment the Bank concluded that it would be necessary to approach the problem of inadequate economic management on a systematic and sustained basis, and preparations for providing training began.'[55] On 15 March 1955, the Bank announced the establishment of the Economic Development Institute (EDI) in Washington.[56] Since then training in the Bank has greatly expanded.

In particular, the World Bank is increasingly supporting 'project-related training' as part of its 'continuing effort to strengthen borrowers' institutions and to eliminate developmental constraints caused by a lack of trained manpower.'[57] The Bank recently announced that 'training in management at all levels, and for all sectors will have a high priority.'[58] And in pursuance of this objective it has offered assistance to set up and/or strengthen administrative training institutions in Malaysia, Nigeria, Ghana, Indonesia, Thailand and other countries.[59]

There is no UN agency now which is not involved in some training activity or the other. Training is an important preoccupation of practically all of them.[60] Apart from the World Bank, other agencies which are concerned with training include DTCD, ILO, FAO, UNESCO, UNIDO, and WHO. Several training institutions have also sprung up directly under the aegis of the UN agencies.[61] Training is emerging as an important component in most technical assistance programmes.[62]

TRAINING AND DEVELOPMENT PROCESS

This rapid growth of development training has produced results which some believe are encouraging. But there are others who think that training has not lived up to its promise. Indeed, one urgent issue in training currently is related to its own effectiveness.[63] What impact do all these training institutions and training programmes have on the performance level of development administrators?

Does training in effect lead to better management of the development plans? Are returns from investments into this enterprise sufficient?

There are many who genuinely believe that if only the personnel could be trained adequately development will proceed smoothly along its course. Undoubtedly, a properly organised training effort should be able to produce the desired results. But quite obviously not all such expectations can be realised where training is undertaken without a thorough knowledge of what exactly is involved in the process.

Lately, there have been some voices of disappointment. Expressing this dissatisfaction with training, Lynton and Pareek noted that 'Complaints are growing about its ineffectiveness and waste. The training apparatus and its costs have multiplied but not the benefits.'[64]

Discussing some of the deficiencies in training, A R Hoyle noted:

> ... Today in the mid-1970s there are many dozens of institutes and schools of public administration operating both in the developed and developing countries and some thousands of academic and professional training officers who devote their efforts to provide the administrative capabilities. But the disillusion which is felt about development efforts in general has not spared training and at a recent large development conference one speaker referred to the training schools and institutions as a disaster area.[65]

Bernard Schaffer does not think that training provided by the training institutions can hope to achieve its objective of adequately equipping the personnel for their new role in promoting development. He is clearly opposed to this manner of training which he disparagingly calls 'trainingism'.[66]

However, such views on training are not shared widely. Disagreeing with the general criticism of training, a UN document on development administration noted:

> A number of persons have criticized the establishment of training institutions and national institutes of public administration on the ground that civil servants can better acquire administrative capability through apprenticeship than through formal training.

Up to now, none of these critics has succeeded in presenting a convincing case. By and large, national institutes of public administration, staff colleges and similar training institutions have made important contributions towards improving the quality of civil servants and enhancing administrative capability:[67]

Perhaps even the severest critics of training will readily admit that 'While training cannot guarantee success, its absence greatly increases the likelihood of failure.'[68] In actual fact most experts see increasing relevance of training to the developmental tasks. The growing popularity of training as an essential input in the development process is a clear testimony of its usefulness. Reflecting on his years with the World Bank, Eugene R Black made this observation in 1976:

I think we did a lot of good things in the World Bank. There are a lot of countries that would be much poorer than they are if we hadn't financed dams, roads and ports and power twenty years ago. But I sometimes think that the gamble we took in establishing EDI was one of the best things we did to help our member countries over the long run.[69]

This is the clearest admission of the vital role of training in promoting development.

Concerning training two extreme views have thus come to the fore. First, training is the only solution to all problems that confront development administrators. Second, training is totally unproductive. Neither of these views can be fully supported. As Lynton and Pareek put it: 'Training is neither a panacea for all ills, nor is it a waste of time.'[70] It is one of several inputs in the development process. Its basic objective is to equip development administrators for their tasks so that they may become more effective in achieving the development goals.

Both exaggerated expectations from training as well as carping criticism against training seem to be rooted in persisting ignorance regarding the true role of training in the development process. Training certainly needs to be better understood. Emphasising the need for a better appreciation of what training is, Wyn Reilly noted:

Training is surprisingly little understood. Indeed to many public servants it is regarded as a waste of time, money, and manpower. To others it is seen as a panacea, a magic answer to the problems of an inefficient public service. In practice it is neither. It is one of several important means of developing a sound and effective administrative system. Thus, there is a need for a far greater understanding of training in its widest sense and in all its forms: to know when training can help and when it cannot, what type may be appropriate, how to improve its effectiveness, and the reasons why administrative training has produced such disappointing results over the past ten to twenty years.[71]

Without a basic understanding of what training can or cannot do training efforts are unlikely to yield very satisfactory results. It is, therefore, important to be aware of both its potentialities and its limitations.

There is nothing to suggest that efforts to properly understand the true nature of the training process are undertaken everywhere. When planning for training, the limitations inherent in the training process are nowhere given any serious consideration. A common assumption is that a period of training for development personnel should immediately be followed by a period of development at an accelerated pace. Observations from widely different geographic regions tend to confirm the belief, that training does produce a decisive impact on the final outcome of the development process.[72] But the results from training are usually slow in coming. They do not become visible quickly like the results of engineering which are seen in a bridge or a dam. A fact that is not realised adequately is that a change in attitudes and behaviour cannot be easily brought about by training effort alone.[73] Observations of Ronald Dore based on studies of community development in Asia, Africa and Latin America are pertinent to this issue:

> Knowledge and skills can be taught and tailored to the required role; perhaps to some degree, perceptiveness and tact can also be developed by training courses. What training courses do very little about is conscientiousness, commitment and enthusiasm — which is perhaps why they are so little discussed as factors in bureaucratic efficiency (not a profitable field for the highly articulate salesman of the training mystique), but they are ... of the greatest importance particularly for the

efficiency of the field officer working on his own initiative in a village situation.[74]

Often it is not realised that training by itself will not be able to help shape the development process. Training will be effective in producing the desired results only when several other factors, outside its ken, are supportive of what training is striving to achieve. Factors, external to training, influence its outcome far more than is ordinarily imagined.[75] For example, delegation of authority will not occur simply because management training programmes have successfully taught the required managerial skills to junior administrators. Unless organisational philosophy, which hitherto has strongly favoured centralisation of all powers, itself undergoes a change towards decentralisation, management training is unlikely to produce any effect in this direction. Again, where bureaucracy is opposed to change, lack of sufficient development cannot be ascribed to training. Bureaucracy is not policy neutral in all Third World countries. It has its own views on development. If status quo is what suits it best, no matter how many training programmes are undertaken this will make no difference to the development situation.

While training is extremely important to the development process, it would be naive to think of it as a panacea for all troubles that afflict development programmes. Training is no substitute for right development policies and sound development programmes. Further, it has been correctly observed that 'training programmes do not solve such administrative deficiencies as defective administrative structures, cumbersome rules and procedures, lack of resources, and so forth.'[76] Concerning the nature of training, Ali Berkman has made some succinct observations:

> ... training by itself is not and cannot be a panacea and, therefore, it should not be viewed as such. Training does not immediately or automatically produce more productive and effective administrators. More training does not necessarily imply that a more capable group of administrators or managers will emerge. It is generally stated that changing the structure and techniques, though important, cannot bring about improvements unless administrators are also changed. However, the

other side of the argument is no less correct. Changing individuals, though important, cannot by itself substantially improve administrative performances. What I have said so far implies that training is a limited instrument. It is just one piece in the puzzle for improving performance. Other pieces of the puzzle must be secured and put into place.[77]

Often results from training have fallen short of expectations. But reasons for the current disenchantment with training are largely related to the unsatisfactory manner in which most training is conducted.[78] Some years ago a study of development training concluded that 'It has ... become abundantly clear that the majority of training programmes are superficial, rushed, and poorly managed, often establishing a negative attitude at the beginning of the assignment. The end result is a cost to the ... project.'[79]

By and large, the planners of training programmes do not seem to have wholly succeeded in making training relevant to the changing job needs of development administrators. From his experiences in Africa, G O Orewa reports:

Another example of poor planning of training programmes is that the institutions for middle-grade training (such as the agricultural colleges in most English-speaking African countries) have not introduced into their curricula such subjects as district and local development, plan formulation and implementation, farm management, and accounting. The result is that the graduates are as good as their pre-independence forerunners.[80]

Pointing out other deficiencies in the training of development personnel, he continues:

The training of middle-grade personnel such as agricultural, co-operative, and rural development assistants has little or no interdisciplinary approach. They are still trained in their different 'cells' without taking account of the fact that in the field these officers must assist local people in formulating development programmes which embrace several ministries. They must be trained to work as a team with officials of other departments and agencies.

In other regions too, training is still being conducted with no concern for the real development objectives. Commenting on the situation in Southeast Asian countries, John Wong recently noted:

> Conventional training programmes will result in the increased supply of bureaucrats who are no doubt capable of managing ... large-scale show-case development projects, if suitably located in some big urban centres, but who are also likely to lose touch with those at the grass-roots level. The need in the future is for greater supply of dedicated development cadres who are more likely 'organizers' or 'mobilizers', capable of involving the masses in the total development effort.[81]

Until recently training programmes for development administrators do not seem to have received enough attention. This partly explains the poor quality of many training programmes in the past. However, things have lately begun changing for the better. In recent years, training has undergone profound transformations and the effort is continuing to enhance its suitability for meeting the contemporary challenges on the development frontiers. A UN paper notes in this connection:

> Tremendous developments have taken place in the field of training.... Many ideas and concepts in the field of training could help to improve both individual and organizational performance and organizations as a whole. It is now widely accepted that the critical dimension of training and development is to help organizations be more effective in the delivery of goods and services.[82]

If training has been unable to produce the promised results, the effort henceforth must be to improve its performance. The problem cannot be overcome by giving up the training effort. The development challenge calls for more and better training, and not its denigration.

TOWARDS MORE EFFECTIVE TRAINING

However, several changes will be necessary before training begins to make a meaningful contribution to the development process. First, training will need to be included as an important component in all development projects. On development projects the trainer will then need to be included in the interdisciplinary development team on a full-time basis as an expert in his own right.[83] He must have opportunities to work through all the stages of the project cycle. The training expert can render useful service in a variety of ways including: (*a*) identifying training needs for the project, (*b*) selecting those who need to be trained, (*c*) suggesting other institutions where alone specialised training would be possible, and (*d*) conducting training locally as much as possible. The training which he will impart will be more job relevant because of his proximity to the project and the opportunities he has to appreciate better all aspects of its design, execution and maintenance. By helping to improve the performance of the project staff, the training expert will directly contribute to cost reduction and other efficiencies.

If development is to proceed at a faster pace it is of the utmost importance that training be drawn closer to the centres where decisions concerning development are made. Trainers themselves need to see more clearly their role in the development process. Development experts too, need to have a better understanding of the potential of training in promoting their own business. The issue today is not whether training can contribute to development, but rather how its contribution can be made more productive.

Here it may be useful to discuss briefly some of the essential conditions which will favour the growth of development-related training along the right lines, and thereby enable it to play an effective part in shaping the final outcome of the development endeavour. There are some factors which are external to training, while others relate to the capability of training itself. The external factors affecting the training process will be considered first.

Training can be effective only if top level administrators perceive it as relevant to the task of development and extend to it all the support it needs to be able to contribute to the improved performance of development personnel on the job. Pronouncements extolling the value of training in the context of development planning and administration are increasingly heard now. But training does not always get from the higher decision-making levels in the government hierarchy the real support it requires to produce the desired results.[84] This is partly due to the persistence of old notions about training which did not accord training its rightful place in the sphere of development.

Without this support, trainers by themselves are in no position either to correctly determine training needs of the development personnel, or to design truly job relevant curricula. Again, trainers who have no access to information, data and documents in the development agencies can hardly ever produce case studies and other literature suitable for use in the classroom. There are several subjects which can be taught best by development administrators as they alone are knowledgeable about the day-to-day problems on the ground. Hence, success of development-related training is greatly dependent on the extent to which training institutions are able to recruit senior administrators as guest faculty. How closeness to the operating organisation is of critical importance to the training institute will be evident from the following:

EDI is able to infuse its programmes with a high degree of realism due primarily to the fact that the Institute is an integral part of the World Bank, and thus able to draw upon the Bank's experience with development through its lending operations. In addition, consultation with the other departments of the Bank provides insights as to the needs for training in particular countries and sectors.... The EDI draws heavily on Bank operations and experiences in developing a pedagogy which relies on case studies, problem solving, field work and the 'learn by doing' method. The orientation of the programme is towards concrete problems and the application of practical techniques in attempting to solve them. The specificity of EDI's courses and its teaching methods entails in-house preparation of most teaching materials.[85]

Training institutions are wholly dependent on the development agencies for nomination of their officials as participants in the training courses. The right use of trained manpower depends on decisions concerning placement which are made, not in the training institute, but in the organisations at higher levels in the administrative hierarchy. What kind of trainers the training institute has is also dependent on decisions taken at higher levels in the government. And without funds, which must come from the organisations that support the training institute, no training activity is conceivable.

However, it is not impossible to bring about desired changes in the external circumstances. Training has all along enjoyed support in many organisations. Organisations which do not attach enough importance to training and do not think they play an important role in strengthening it can gradually become more supportive of training.

External factors are undoubtedly important to the success of any training endeavour. But even more important is what training itself can do to equip administrators with the knowledge, skills, and attitudes they need to be effective in their difficult development tasks. Demand for the training of development administrators has grown rapidly, but the training capability does not seem to have increased simultaneously. Institution-building for training is a slow process.[86] Strengthening the training capability will require action on several fronts.[87] It is easier to construct buildings and other such facilities, to procure equipment and furniture, to buy books and journals, but these measures alone do not enhance the training capability.

Trainers remain the single, most important training resource. They are in short supply practically everywhere. The development of trainers should therefore, be a matter of top priority in plans that seek to strengthen the overall training capability.[88]

The design of curricula which takes account of the work that administrators actually do and should do is an important matter.[89] However, this area has been neglected. A properly designed curricula can have a perceptible effect on the performance level of development administrators. Trainers need to devote more attention to this task.

The question of teaching materials is an important one. Trainers tend to follow the easier path — many trainers unhesitatingly use borrowed materials in their classrooms. Being of limited relevance to the job needs of participants, such materials, especially the case studies, do not really contribute much to new learning. The value of good training materials needs to be appreciated far more than has been the case till now.

Often trainers prefer to have minimal contacts with the organisations and administrators whose training needs they are supposed to meet. If training is to be responsive to the real job needs of the development personnel, trainers must first understand what the job involves and what the exact training needs are for that job. This is possible only when they come out of their isolation and design programmes to suit the specific requirements of each situation.

Through their own efforts, trainers can greatly strengthen the capability of training to help produce administrators required for the tasks connected with the planning and administration of development. But all that could have been done to improve the quality of training has perhaps not been attempted yet. Here, trainers face some very challenging opportunities.[90]

Conclusion

In recent years, investments of scarce resources into development plans and projects designed specifically to benefit the poorer sections of society have been of a fairly high order. As development in the Third World is increasingly seen as a matter of the highest priority, this trend is certain to continue further.[91] Such changes are bound to overstretch the present scarce administrative resources in these countries. Fortunately, the expenditure on training and development efforts is an infinitesimally small fraction of the total costs on development projects. Still matters related to administrative development as part of the overall development process do not seem to be receiving enough attention. However, unless administrators on whose shoulders will fall this heavy burden of planning and implementing the development plans are adequately equipped for the job, development plans are unlikely to succeed in realising all their objectives. Indeed, there is now every reason to support training as an essential input in the development process and to see that it becomes progressively more productive.

NOTES AND REFERENCES

1. David Morawetz. 1977. *Twenty-five Years of Economic Development 1950 to 1975.* Washington DC: The World Bank. Also see, *World Development Report, 1978.* Washington DC: The World Bank, August 1978.
2. Samuel Paul. 1982. *Managing Development Programs.* Boulder, Colorado: Westview Press. Also see, Milton Easman and John Montgomery.The Administration of Human Development. *In* Peter T. Knight (ed.). 1980. *Implementing Programs of Human Development.* (World Bank Staff Working Paper No. 403, July 1980). Washington DC: The World Bank.

3. Merilee S. Grindle (ed.). 1980. *Politics and Policy Implementation in the Third World.* Princeton, N.J.: Princeton University Press. See, George Honadle and Rudi Klauss (eds.). 1979. *International Development Administration.* New York: Praeger. Also see, G. Shabbir Cheema (ed.). 1981. *Institutional Dimensions of Regional Development.* Singapore: Maruzen Asia.

4. ICOMP. 1979. *Developing Programme Implementation Capabilities in Population Organisations.* Kamati, Rizal, Philippines: ICOMP.

5. David K. Leonard. 1977. *Reaching the Peasant Farmer: Organization Theory and Practice in Kenya.* Chicago: University of Chicago Press. Also see, Elliott R. Morss *et al.* 1977. *Strategies for Small Farmer Development.* Vol. I. Boulder, Colorado: Westview Press.

6. Milton J. Easman. Popular Participation in Development Administration. *Journal of Comparative Administration,* Vol. 3, No. 3, November 1971, pp. 358-82.

7. Five cases of successful projects are described in David C. Korten. Community Organisation and Rural Development: A Learning Process Aproach. *Public Administration Review,* Vol. 40, No. 5, September-October 1980, pp. 490-511.

8. Samuel Paul. 1980. *Strategic Management of Public Programmes.* Ahmedabad: Indian Institute of Management (mimeo).

9. Richard Heaver. 1982. *Bureaucratic Politics and Incentives in the Management of Rural Development.* Washington DC: The World Bank (Staff Working Paper No. 537). Also see, Peter Bowden. Administrative Management: The Missing Ingredient in the Bank's Development Programs. *In* Margaret Wolfson. 1981. *Aid Implementation and Administrative Capacity in Upper Volta.* Paris: Development Centre of the OECD.

10. Edward A. Kieloch. Some Administrative Shortcomings of Intensive Agricultural Development Programme. *Indian Journal of Public Administration,* Vol. XIII, No. 3, July-September 1967.

11. Shanker N. Acharya. Perspectives and Problems of Development in Sub-Saharan Africa. *World Development,* Vol. 9, No. 2, February 1981, p. 126.

12. Referring to the problems of public administration and management in Western Africa, the World Development Report, 1980 noted: 'Embryonic at the time of independence, public administration in the Region's countries has been greatly strained by the growing complexity of economic management.' *World Development Report, 1980.* Washington: The World Bank. P. 36.

13. Alec McCallum. Why Improve the Organisation and Administration of Agricultural Development? *Improving the Organisation and Administration of Agricultural Development in the Near East.* Report of a Regional Expert Consultation held in Nicosia, Cyprus, December 1980. Rome: FAO, 1981. Pp. 20-25.

14. E.J. Berg. Structural Transformation Versus Gradualism: Recent Economic Development in Ghana and Ivory Coast. *In* P. Foster and A.R. Zolberg (eds.). 1971. *Ghana and Ivory Coast: Perspectives in Modernization.* Chicago: University of Chicago Press.

15. Peter Bowden. How Project Assistance Adds to Third World Woes. *Report: News and Views from the World Bank.* November-December 1979. Washington DC: The World Bank. Pp. 3-4.

16. Report of Group on Administrative Arrangements and Personnel Policies in Tribal Areas. New Delhi: Ministry of Home Affairs, Government of India. 1979. P. 1.

17. Proceedings of the Inter-regional Seminar on Organisation and Administration of Development Planning Agencies. Kiev Ukrainian Soviet Socialist Republic, 16-25 October 1972. Vol. I. Report and General Technical Papers. New York: United Nations, Department of Economic and Social Affairs, Public Administration Division. 1971. Sales Publication No. E 71.II. H.3. P. 37.

18. *Public Administration in the Second United Nations Development Decade.* Report of the Second Meeting of Experts. New York: United Nations, Department of Economic and Social Affairs, Public Administration Division. 1971. Sales Publication No. E 71.II. H. 3. P. 27.

19. David C. Korten. Toward a Technology for Managing Social Development. *In* David C. Korten (ed.). 1979. *Population and Social Development Management: A Challenge for Management Schools.* Caracas, Venezuela: IESA. Pp. 20-50.

20. Sridath Ramphal. 1979. *One World to Share: Selected Speeches of the Commonwealth Secretary-General 1975-79.* Oxford: Oxford University Press. P. 441. From the valedictory address at the 18th World Management Congress held in New Delhi, 8 December 1978.

21. Harry T. Toulmin and M.R. Chanram S. Chandradhat. Improving Public Management in Newly Developing Countries. *In* Richard J. Ward (ed.). 1967. *The Challenge of Development: Theory and Practice.* Chicago: Aldine Publishing Company. P. 133.

22. Alec McCallum. Unsnarling the Bureaucracy: Devolution and Rural Development. *CERES,* Vol. 13, No. 2, March-April 1980, p. 36.

23. Anthony Bottrall. Technology and Management in Irrigated Agriculture. *ODI Review,* (2), 1978, p. 47.

24. Allen D. Jedlicka. 1977. *Organization for Rural Development: Risk-Taking and Appropriate Technology.* New York: Praeger Publishers. P. xiv.

25. Martin C. Evans *et al.* 1979. *Sector Paper on Agriculture and Rural Development.* Manila: Asian Development Bank. Pp. 42-43.

26. Martin C. Evans *et al.* 1979. *Sector Paper on Agriculture and Rural Development.* Manila: Asian Development Bank. P. 16.

27. Keith Griffin. Economic Development in a Changing World. *World Development,* 9 (3), March 1981, 221-26.

28. Improving administrative performance for development is a subject of great current interest. See T.N. Chaturvedi. 1980. *Administrative Performance.* Lucknow: University of Lucknow. (This is the first Professor V.K.N. Memorial Lecture organised by the Indian Public Administration Association at Lucknow University on 7 April 1980). Also see, United Nations 1979. *Handbook on Improvement of Administration.* New York: United Nations.

29. From a report on the XVIIIth International Congress of Administrative Sciences, Madrid, 30 June-4 July 1980. *International Review of Administrative Sciences,* Vol. XLVI, No. 3, 1980, p. 302.

30. Cf. It is a sound advice for governments in the developing countries that 'the implementation capacity for the institutional framework of agricultural development should be increased.' See. M. Riad El Ghonemy. 1979. *Agrarian Reform and Rural Development in the Near East.* Rome: FAO (RNEA). P. 17.

31. Department of Technical Cooperation for Development. 1979. *Organizational Systems for National Planning.* New York: United Nations. Sales Publication No. E. 79. II. H.2. See in this connection. Arturo Israel. Toward Better Project

Management. *Finance and Development*, Vol. 15, No. 1, March 1978, pp. 27-30.

32. Paul Harrison. 1980. *The Third World Tomorrow*. Harmondsworth: Penguin Books Ltd. P. 342. Also see. Paul Harrison. 1981. *Inside the Third World*. (Second edition). Harmondsworth: Penguin Books Ltd.

33. Paul Harrison. 1980. *The Third World Tomorrow*. Harmondsworth: Penguin Books Ltd. P. 23.

34. A recent publication on this growing subject is Kamla Bhasin and Vimala R. (eds.). 1980. *Readings on Poverty, Politics and Development*. Rome: FAO (Office of the Coordinator FFHC/AD).

35. Hari Mohan Mathur. *Rural Development in Traditional Societies: An Anthropological Perspective*. Paper prepared for the Symposium on Rural Development in South Asia, Intercongress IUAES, Amsterdam, April 1981.

36. Cocoyoc Declaration particularly emphasises the development of man. 'The purpose of development should not be to develop things, but to develop man.' (UN Document A/C2/292 of November 1974). Freedom is emphasised in Soejatmoko. 1979. *Development and Freedom*. Ishizaka Memorial Lecture.

37. Sartaj Aziz. Clearing the Path Towards International Cooperation. *South: The Third World Magazine*, March 1981, p. 18.

38. The typical functions and responsibilities of development administrators are discussed in Kwame Adjei. *Some Problems and Existing African Experiences in the Field of In-Service Training for Senior Management and Administrative Public Personnel*. Paper presented to the UN Expert Group Meeting on Curricula Design for Management Development. Arusha, Tanzania, 20-24 July 1981.

39. Michael Bentil. *Opening Remarks* at the UN Expert Group Meeting on Curricula Design for Management Development, Arusha, Tanzania, 20-24 July 1981. (Meeting convened by the UN Development Administration Division, New York). P. 2.

40. *Development Administration: Current Approaches and Trends in Public Administration for National Development*. New York: United Nations, Department of Economic and Social Affairs. 1975. P. 32.

41. Economic and Social Council of the United Nations (ECOSOC) Resolution 1978/6 of 10 May 1978.

42. *Development Administration Newsletter*, No. 65, January-June 1980, p. 11. See, Public Administration and Finance for Development in the 1980s: The Fifth Meeting of Experts on the United Nations Programme in Public Administration and Finance. Pp. 10-15.

43. Irving Swerdlow and Marcus Ingle (eds.). 1974. *Public Administration Training for the Less Developed Countries*. Syracuse: Maxwell School of Citizenship and Public Affairs.

44. In this connection see, Charles V. Kidd. 1980. *Manpower Policies for the Use of Science and Technology in Development*. New York: Pergamon Press. A relevant observation here is:

> ... manpower development is fundamental because without trained people, no other factor of production works at all. Facilities and equipment are useless without trained people to operate them. Technology is developed, transferred, and adapted by trained people. For these reasons, conscious attention to the training of people should be a prominent part of every strategy of development. (P. ix.)

45. Dag Hammerskjold. *An Address to the International Law Association.* Montreal, 30 May 1956. Quoted in the announcement for the Dag Hammerskjold Fellowship 1964 offered by the Graduate School of Public and International Affairs, University of Pittsburg.

46. *Education: Sector Policy Paper.* (Third edition). Washington DC: The World Bank. April 1980. P. 49.

47. *World Development Report, 1980.* Washington DC. 1980. P. 76.

48. Irving Swerdlow and Marcus Ingle. Introduction. *In* Irving Swerdlow and Marcus Ingle (eds.). 1974. *Public Administration Training for the Less Developeu Countries.* Syracuse: Maxwell School of Citizenship and Public Affairs. P. 1.

49. *The Training Division.* (A brochure). New Delhi: Government of India, Department of Personnel and Administrative Reforms, Training Division. 1978.

50. *Improving the Organisation and Administration of Agricultural Development in the Near East.* Report of a Regional Expert Consultation held in Nicosia, Cyprus, December 1980. Rome: FAO. 1981. P. 9.

51. Irving Swerdlow and Marcus Ingle. Preface. *In* Irving Swerdlow and Marcus Ingle (eds.). 1974. *Public Administration Training for the Less Developed Countries.* Syracuse: Maxwell School of Citizenship and Public Affairs. P. vii.

52. See, Report of the Inter-regional Seminar on the Development of Senior Administrators in the Public Service of Developing Countries, Geneva, 19-20 August 1968. Vol. I. Report and Technical Papers. New York: United Nations. 1969.

53. Milton J. Easman. Administrative Doctrine and Developmental Needs. *In* E. Philip Morgan (ed.). 1974. *Administration of Change in Africa: Essays in the Theory and Practice of Development Administration in Africa.* New York Dunellen Publishing Company Inc. P. 22.

54. This growth is reflected in the size of the published directories of training insti . tions. One such directory is *Training in Public Administration: A Director Commonwealth Resources.* London: Commonwealth Secretariat. 1978. 'ı growth is also reflected in the membership of professional associations, suɪ . as the Association of Development Research and Training ʼɪnstitutes of Asia and the Pacific (ADIPA) with its new headquarters at Kuala Lumpur. See, *ADIPA: A Directory of Members.*Compiled by Elizabeth W. Ng. Hongkong: Centre of Asian Studies, University of Hongkong. 1979.

55. John H. Adler. The Economic Development Institute of the World Bank. *International Development Review*, Vol. V, No. 1, March 1963.

56. Bank Establishes Economic Development Institute. Press Release. *A M Newspapers.* Friday, 11 March 1955. Washington DC: The World Bank.

57. *The World Bank and Education Projects.* March 1979. Washington DC: The World Bank. P. 4.

58. *Education: Sector Policy Papers.* (Third edition). Washington DC: The World Bank. April 1980. P. 49.

59. See, *Malaysia: Fifth Educational Project Staff Appraisal Report* (Mimeographed Report No. 2082-MA). Washington DC: The World Bank. 1979.

60. For some training activities of the International Labour Organisation (ILO) see a recent booklet, *Effective Managers for Development: The Management Development Programme of the ILO.* Geneva: ILO. (Undated, may be it was brought out in 1980.)

61. Among such institutes are: United Nations Institute for Training and Research (UNITAR), New York; Economic Development Institute of the World Bank (EDI), Washington; United Nations Centre for Regional Development (UNCRD), Nagoya; International Centre for Public Enterprises in Developing Countries (ICPE), Lubjliyana; United Nations Asian and Pacific Development Centre (UN APDC), Kuala Lumpur; etc.

62. One UN document exhorts: 'All efforts should be made... to continue and expand technical assistance programmes including... management development of national personnel of the developing countries in the light of their special development requirements.' *United Nations Programme of Action on the Establishment of New International Economic Order.*

63. B.L. Jacobs and Bernard Schaffer. Training for Improved Performance by Public Service: An Assessment. *Inter-regional Seminar on Major Administrative Reforms in Developing Countries.* Vol. II. Technical Papers (Part One) Falmer, Brighton, United Kingdom of Great Britain and Northern Ireland. 25 October-2 November 1971. New York: United Nations. 1973. Pp. 141-51. Also see in this connection, Jake Jacobs. The Evaluation of Fellowships and Training Programmes. *Workshop on Methodology and Techniques for the Evaluation of Fellowship and Training Programmes.* UNESCO Headquarters. 24-28 November 1981. Paris: UNESCO, Fellowships Division, Cooperation for Development and External Relations Sector. (Annex IV 1-15).

64. Rolf P. Lynton and Udai Pareek. 1967. *Training for Development.* Homewood, Illinois: The Dorsey Press. P. 3.

65. A.R. Hoyle. Some Deficiencies in the Training for Senior Administrators of Developing Countries. *International Review of Administrative Sciences,* Vol. XL, No. 4, 1974, p. 329.

66. Bernard Schaffer (ed.). 1974. *Administrative Training and Development: A Comparative Study of East Africa, Zambia, Pakistan and India.* New York: Praeger Publishers. See Chapter 1, Introduction: The Ideas and Institutions of Training, and Chapter 8, Conclusion: The Situations of Training.

67. *Development Administration: Current Approaches and Trends in Public Administration for National Development.* New York: United Nations. 1975. P. 87.

68. *Training for Agricultural Project Management: Papers from a Commonwealth Workshop.* Colombo, Sri Lanka, 1979. London: Commonwealth Secretariat. 1980. P. 9.

69. Eugene R. Black. EDI at Twenty. *In* Michael L. Hoffman. 1978. *EDI/20: Memoir of a Fellowship.* Washington: The Economic Development Institute of the World Bank. P. 69.

70. Rolf P. Lynton and Udai Pareek. 1967. *Training for Development.* Homewood, Illinois: The Dorsey Press. P. 4.

71. Wyn Reilly. 1979. *Training Administrators for Development.* London: Heinemann. Pp. 2-3.

72. Samuel Paul. 1981. Beyond Investment: Some Lessons from Development Programmes. *Economic and Political Weekly* (Review of Management), Vol. XVI, No. 48, 28 November 1981, pp. M 130-40. Writing on successful programmes selected from different parts of the Third World, Samuel Paul observed that 'The role of training in the development of people was prominent in all programmes.' (P. M 135).

73. Hari Mohan Mathur. Some Civil Service Attitudes Inappropriate in the Development Context: Using Training as a Correctional Device. *In Training for Attitudinal Change: Proceedings of the Annual Conference on Training.* New Delhi: Government of India, Training Division. 1976.

74. Ronald Dore. Introduction. *In* Ronald Dore and Zoe Mars (eds.). 1981. *Community Development: Comparative Case Studies in India, the Republic of Korea, Mexico and Tanzania.* London: Croom Helm and Paris: UNESCO. P. 42.

75. Milton J. Easman. New Directions in Rural Development: The Changing Role of Officials. *Training Strategies for Integrated Rural Development.* Kuala Lumpur: Asian and Pacific Development Administration Centre, 1979. 'Indeed, a formal training is likely to be ineffectual unless the work environment rewards and compels new forms of behaviour. More important than formal training, therefore, are changes in the work environment.' (P. 69).

76. Carlos P. Ramos. Identifying Training Needs and Methods in the Context of Management Development. *In* Inayatullah (ed.). 1975. *Management Training for Development: The Asian Experience.* Kuala Lumpur: Asian Centre for Development Administration. P. 234.

77. Ali Berkman. Comments. *In* Irving Swerdlow and Marcus Ingle (eds.). 1974. *Public Administration Training for the Less Developed Countries.* Syracuse: Maxwell School of Citizenship and Public Affairs. P. 69.

78. For a discussion of major weaknesses in current training programmes see, Martin J. Boodhoo. Training Systems and Curricula for Public Enterprise Management in Commonwealth Countries. *Training Systems and Curricula Development for Public Enterprise Management: Recommendations for National Policies and Programmes by an Expert Group.* Reduit, Mauritius, 23-26 April 1979. London: Commonwealth Secretariat. 1979.

79. Thomas F. Trail. 1968. *Education of Development Technicians: A Guide to Training Programmes.* New York: Frederick A Praeger. P. X.

80. G.O. Orewa. Some Aspects of Development Planning and Administration in Africa. *In* E. Philip Morgan (ed.). 1974. *The Administration of Change in Africa.* New York: Dunellen. P. 115.

81. John Wong. 1979. *ASEAN Economies in Perspective: A Comparative Study of Indonesia, Malaysia, the Philippines, Singapore and Thailand.* London: Macmillan. P. 129.

82. *The Role of Training of Trainers in Administrative Development.* A Working Paper prepared in the Division of Public Administration and Finance, United Nations, for the Inter-regional Workshop on the Training of Trainers, Vienna, 6-12 July 1976.

83. Richard W. Van Wagenen. Training as an Element in Bank Group Projects. *Finance and Development,* September 1972, pp. 34-39.

84. Bernard Schaffer has observed: 'Nor is there anything in the traditions of higher administration to build up a commitment to training by the top men.' (P. 47). See, Bernard Schaffer (ed.). 1974. *Administrative Training and Development: A Comparative Study of East Africa, Zambia, Pakistan and India.* New York: Praeger.

85. *The Experience of the Economic Development Institute in the Field of Training* EDI, 20 January 1978. Washington: EDI of the World Bank. 1978.

86. Jacques Roumani. 1979. *The World Bank and Institution-Building: Experience*

and Directions for Future Work. Washington: World Bank. Also see, Milan Kubr (ed.). 1982. *Managing a Management Development Institution.* Geneva: International Labour Office (Management Development Series No. 18).

87. Ravi Mathai, Udai Pareek and T.V. Rao (eds.). 1977. *Institution-Building in Education and Research: From Stagnation to Self-Renewal.* New Delhi: All India Management Association.

88. *Report and Recommendations of the Inter-regional Workshop on the Training of Trainers,* Vienna, 6–12 July 1976. New York: UN Division of Public Administration and Finance (mimeographed).

89. UN, Department of Technical Cooperation for Development Administration Division recently organised an Expert Group Meeting on Curricula Design for Management Development in Arusha, Tanzania, 20–24 July 1981.

90. One example of how trainers are developing innovative approaches is George H. Honadle and John P. Hannah. 1982. Management Performance for Rural Development: Packaged Training or Capacity Building. *Public Administration and Development,* Vol. 2, 1982, 295-307.

91. *North-South: A Programme for Survival.* The Report of the Independent Commission on International Development under the Chairmanship of Willy Brandt. London: Pan Books. 1980.

Rural Development in Traditional Societies

As mankind reaches out for the stars, there remain on the home planet, earth, large numbers of the poor who are unable to live a fully human life. Indeed, the Third World today is characterised by the pervasive degrading poverty of its millions.[1] Development which all these years should have focused on the poor seems simply to have bypassed them.

The World Bank has recently estimated the number of people living in absolute poverty in the Third World at around 780 millions.[2] Half of them are in South Asia. The other half lives in East and Southeast Asia, sub-Saharan Africa, Latin America, North Africa and the Middle East. Roughly 80 per cent of the poor live in the countryside mostly as small farmers and landless labourers. Poverty is thus an essentially rural phenomenon.

Absolute poverty, in the words of McNamara, is 'a condition of life so characterized by malnutrition, illiteracy, disease, squalic surroundings, high infant mortality, and low expectancy as to be beneath any reasonable definition of human decency.'[3] However formidable, poverty and underdevelopment are in some ways easier to conquer today than was the case earlier. 'Yet for all man's potential we appear to have constructed political systems that make an attack on poverty more difficult than it was in the past.'[4] Thus eradication of poverty is the greatest challenge facing mankind today.

People in the developed countries perhaps cannot fully comprehend the true nature of this widespread rural poverty in the Third World.[5] Acknowledging that this really is so, the Brandt Commission report says, 'Few people in the North have any detailed conception of the extent of poverty in the Third World or of the forms which it takes.'[6] Partly, this is explainable by the fact that it is not easy to describe poverty in all its dimensions. Statistics do not help here; facts and figures do not tell the whole story. Indeed, language is a poor vehicle to convey fully the essence of human misery.

The Challenge of Rural Poverty

It is to alleviate this widespread poverty in the rural areas that nationally as well as internationally organised development efforts have mainly been undertaken in recent years. The number and variety of development programmes that seek to reach the rural poor have rapidly multiplied.[7] High priority is now given to programmes that seek improvement in the productive capabilities of, and the public services for, the poor especially those living in the rural areas.

Development of the rural poor is emerging as the main target of all current rural development efforts. Rural development, as defined by the World Bank, is simply 'a strategy designed to improve the economic and social life of a particular group of people — the rural poor.'[8] The strategy of launching a direct attack on mass poverty has now become widely acceptable.[9]

However, experience with rural development has brought to light cases of both successes and failures.[10] Unfortunately, the number of successful development cases reported remains small. It is the haltingly moving programmes and projects that dominate the rural development scene. It would appear that poverty has firmly withstood the attacks made against it so far. Instead of retreating, rural poverty seems to have made further advances.

On the basis of a study utilising data from 74 developing countries, Adelman and Morris came to the conclusion that development has only made things worse for the poor. They state that 'hundreds of millions of desperately poor throughout the world have been hurt rather than helped by economic development.'[11] Studies recently conducted in rural Asia tend to confirm that the standard of living of the absolute poor has declined over time.[12] Expected benefits from the growth process as measured in terms of GNP seem not to be spreading widely to cover all sections of the society. By and large, the poor have tended to remain poor.

It is now becoming increasingly clear that this deadlock in

development is attributable to the sole preoccupation of the planners with issues related to accelerating the pace of economic growth.[13] Simultaneously it is also being recognised that the socio-cultural dimension which has not received sufficient attention in the earlier planning exercises is an important factor in the development equation.[14] Development is a complex, multi-layered subject. Current rural development literature is replete with stories of how well-meaning development projects frequently fail to reach the target population.[15] Further, as anthropological studies of the development process show, this is not purely accidental. Many such rural projects which end in failure go against the deeply ingrained social and cultural patterns and processes.[16]

If pastoral nomads are given agricultural lands to settle in the newly irrigated desert region and expected to change over to a sedantarised way of living which irrigated farming system demands, development will, at best, proceed at a slower pace. If efforts are made to increase enrolment in rural primary schools during the busy agricultural season when children are most needed at the farms to lend a helping hand to their parents, the results are bound to be disappointing. If training programmes to improve skills in certain crafts are directed at men in societies where women actually do the work, there is unlikely to be any considerable improvement in the situation.

Improving Access of the Poor to Public Services

Reaching to the poor has proved to be a much more complex task than was visualised earlier.[17] Planners and administrators here are on unfamiliar ground. There is no previous experience to guide them in their operations.[18] Often they are, therefore, unable both to anticipate the socio-cultural hurdles which arise during the plan implementation phase, and to try to overcome them.

Since the human factors in rural development process have not traditionally been accorded due importance, knowledge in these matters has not developed to the required degree.[19] An Asian Development Bank document recently noted that 'very little is known about the socio-economic milieu in which the poor live and operate.'[20] Frequently the planners of rural development make assumptions about village life and the rural poor which are not always tenable.

Often differences among villages in different regions are not considered significant enough. Villages across regions are thought of as an entity possessing certain common characteristics. However, the fact is that even neighbouring villages manifest differences in many important respects. On the basis of his study, Charles A Murray has recounted the readily visible differences among neighbouring villages in Thailand:

Thai villages indeed differ, as any villager will confirm. Some are tranquil; some have a history of feuds. Some are pious and sober; others have a jug of moonshine under every porch and card games every night. Some villages are proud of themselves, and proclaim that they grow the sweetest tamarind or the biggest durian or the most beautiful women in the country. Other villages are a collection of houses with only a name for a common bond, and no pride at all.

Some villages are interminably curious. If a stranger strolls through them, he will be asked at every second house to stop and chat. In another village just down the road, he can walk for an hour with hardly a greeting. If he stays for a few days, some villages will prove to be ceremonious in their treatment of him, others relaxed and unbuttoned, still others suspicious and aloof.

Some villages are clean, others are dirty. Some are spread out over several kilometres, each house hidden from its neighbours. In others, the houses will be crammed together until their porches touch.

Villages are unpredictable. In one village located a few minutes away from a large town, the visitor still has to explain that the world is round; in another, hours from anywhere, the headman will let him listen to a recording of a Mozart quintet, played on a wind-up Victrola.

But most importantly, some villages seem able to solve their problems while others cannot. Some villages are victimized by conmen, their daughters seduced by recruiters from the city's brothels, plagued by police looking for a rake-off, unable to stop the river from flooding the fields every year — while other villages ignore the conmen, keep out the recruiters, get the district office to rein in the police, and build an earthen dam to hold back the river.

All of them are everyday aspects of life, and together they

shape the quality of life in the village. There are limits, of course. An impoverished village living on the edge of starvation is an unpleasant place to live regardless of any other conditions. But given a typical (for Thailand) level of natural resources, the nature of the village — its gestalt, if you will — is a crucial factor in determining whether its inhabitants' daily existence is generally pleasant or generally unpleasant.

It is perhaps the most commonly overlooked fact of life in developing countries.[21]

Rural development plans which are unable to capture the intervention-relevant essence of these differences in villages cannot hope to fully aid in their development.

The community development programme of the 1950s was based on the premise that the village communities were closely knit, harmonious entities and that in response to exhortations of the community development officials the people from villages would come out to build roads, schools, wells, tanks and other community assets. It was believed that people would work together and equitably share in the benefits of development. Planners visualised a 'Panchayati Raj' and under the scheme of democratic decentralisation devolved responsibility for local development on the village leaders. What happened to the Panchayati Raj which was introduced with great fanfare to bring development and people close together was described some time ago in the following terms:

When Panchayati Raj came great hopes were aroused and it was expected that Panchayats would be in a position to involve all the people in local efforts to build the village community on a pattern in which disparities would quickly vanish. But the people who were elected to the Panchayats and the people who failed to get elected later ranged themselves into strong warring factions, usually along the caste lines. Soon they became so busy in fighting among themselves — not always on issues relating to improvement of the village life — that the task of development simply got relegated into the background. In fact this situation did not allow much development to occur, and where development did occur it only benefited the powerful and the influential members of the Panchayat or their relatives and friends. The benefits did not trickle down to the lowliest in the village.[22]

Failure to perceive village life as it is with distinct caste groups, forms of cooperative living, factions and their frequent fights has led to a situation where planning is divorced from reality on the ground.

Among the planners a widely held belief is that peasants do not like to change and that they offer resistance to whatever plans are made for their development. Some have even gone to the extent of branding them as lazy, stupid, incapable of either attaining or enjoying higher standards of living. According to a common stereotype, 'farmers are ultra-conservative individuals, steeped in tradition, hemmed in by custom, lacking in motivation and incentive, captives of age-old methods, and lacking in ability to make wise decisions.'[23]

To those who blamed the conservative farmers for the slow development of agriculture only a few years ago, the current agitations of the same conservative farmers for more fertilisers, water, electricity, etc., must be quite perplexing. Anthropological studies have firmly established that farmers have all these years been wrongly characterised as lazy, conservative, bound up by traditions and superstitions.[24] Such characterisation has been and continues to be helpful only to planners and administrators — they are absolved from responsibilities for the project failures.

Evidence on the adoption of innovations among farmers from different parts of the world seems to indicate that farmers are willing to change if advantages of the recommended practices can be conclusively demonstrated. They are, in fact, vocal in demanding changes. On the other hand, it is the dominant groups and individuals who work hard to see that the poor farmers do not go far ahead on the road to development. They are always looking for opportunities to exploit the situation to their own exclusive advantage.

Development affects diverse groups differently. Its avowed aim is to benefit the poorer groups most of all. Therefore, the rich are not likely to view the process favourably. As they stand to lose once the development process starts, their entire effort is to ensure that at least the *status quo* is not upset. On the basis of his studies, W F Wertheim concludes that the real obstacles to development come not from the poor who are willing to change, but from the rich who are opposed to change.[25]

It is the inadequate understanding of village life which primarily accounts for poor planning and slow implementation of most rural development programmes. Unfortunately, planners and administrators do not even have a desire to know more about the rural poor. Often it is stated that while some knowledge of the village life may be necessary for experts from abroad, this would be unnecessary for local experts as they are expected to know all about life in their own countries.

The fallacy of this argument is increasingly becoming apparent. Possibly, the local expert may know something about villages in his area, but he cannot be expected to automatically possess complete knowledge of village life relevant to his work as a rural development planner and administrator. In India, a country of continental diversity, the differences in lifestyle in various regions are so marked that even an expert on rural life cannot be expected to have knowledge of the entire country.

In addition to this, most planners and administrators in the Third World come from an urban background. Their world and the world of the rural poor are quite dissimilar. Therefore, there is no escape from the fact that unless those responsible for development of the poor are aware of their conditions, the programmes will miss their targets completely. In most Third World countries, as the World Development Report, 1980 points out 'administration is not properly geared to identifying the people to be served, increasing their access to services, adapting services until they are appropriate, delivering them efficiently and observing (and reacting to) the public's response.'[26] This sequence requires administrators who can gain confidence of the rural poor and who would be willing to learn from them. Clearly, there is tremendous scope for strengthening administrative capability in this direction.[27]

Reluctance in Participation

On the part of the poor there are no compulsions of any kind to stay poor.[28] If they could help it, they would certainly like to get rid of their poverty. Why, then does poverty still persist? A simple answer is that the poor cannot lift themselves above the poverty line through their own individual efforts. The odds are heavily against the poor on this battlefront.

The poor live in highly stratified societies, with clearly demarcated class, caste and other groupings, involved in the pursuit of their own interests. The system has been so designed that the higher groups are able to retain their socio-economic power. Further, the poor are prevented by religion, tradition, and other social forces to unite and to challenge the established position of affluent groups.[29] This is true of most Third World countries.

Governments are anxious to see that benefits from public services begin reaching the poor directly, and that the poor are actively involved in programmes designed to promote their development. However, the poor are prevented from enjoying the benefits of these development programmes. Many factors account for this situation.

First, the rural poor do not enthusiastically come forward to receive the development assistance which the development personnel offer them. At the back of their minds are old memories of officials who, in the past, visited them only to collect taxes. Many people in the interior rural areas are still not prepared to believe that the officials can ever play a different role, that of promoting their development.[30] Bailey has sketched the peasant distrust of officials in a very candid manner. Like officials, the peasants too have their stereotypes. The peasants view the officials including those from development agencies as 'unpredictable, unsympathetic, ignorant and immeasurably powerful. "They" do not understand "our" problems.'[31]

Second, the rural elites do not want the rural poor to come into contact with the officials. As agricultural modernisation proceeds, the need for farmers to have increased contacts with the outside agencies has rapidly grown. Inputs and services which public agencies offer the farmers are not very abundant. Hence, the rich and the powerful in the village are keen to monopolise the contacts with outside government agencies and personnel. Joan P Mencher has observed: 'It is striking how hard the majority of panchayat presidents work to try to keep government personnel and others from having too much direct contact with the poor; they obviously have some, but the less the better.'[32]

Finally, there is the question of social distance between the officials and the poor. Often the officials are from higher caste groups, whereas the poor in the village represent the lower caste groups. Thus social background does not allow interaction between the two groups on a basis and with a frequency necessary for development to proceed in full swing. Officials, then, have the option to meet and to work only among the high caste villagers. When that happens it helps development programmes to proceed further. But this partnership of the officials and the elites makes the rural poor more suspicious of the officials, with unfavourable repercussions on the entire development process.[33]

Participation by the poor in the development process has been talked about endlessly, but this does not seem to have been realised except partially and in some favoured show-piece project villages. It is not easy for the poor to organise and to raise their voice against the vested interests that have exploited them and kept them down in their present low positions. A point to remember here is that the poor do not constitute a single category with all the people below a particular income level having a common objective in fighting the affluent. Individually, a majority of the poor is so heavily dependent upon the rich (usually the money-lender), that protest as a way of demanding their share in development may not be considered the most practical thing in the circumstances. John P Powelson says:

> We reach the pessimistic conclusion that the poor are themselves unable to do anything to change this situation, and that the others who might be their advocates, such as the governments or inter-national lending agencies, have political constraints that make them unwilling to make the necessary effort. The poor are destined to remain poor until, largely through their own efforts, they acquire the knowledge and the economic leverage to become rich.[34]

The poor have very little access to information. Often they know almost nothing about the plans and programmes designed only to promote their development. Information systems of the kind that may be of educational value to the rural poor still have not been developed to the required extent.

The way development is designed and administered does not enthuse the poor people. Everything comes from above. In some places tinned food received as aid from the affluent countries for distribution amongst the victims of famine instantly found its way in the food-stores of the bigger cities. The poor have no use for this food; their food habits are very different.

People in the Third World have their own ideas of what constitutes development. These merit careful consideration if the poor are to participate in the development process of their own accord.[35]

Development planning of the top-down kind excludes, not invites, participation of the poor in the development process.

Tradition and Development

For a long time tradition which still remains a dominant factor in the lives of the rural poor in the Third World, has been seen as a factor totally opposed to development and change. Therefore, planners and administrators have tended to minimise its significance in rural development planning and implementation. Difficulties encountered in specifically assisting the development of the poorer groups and in securing their voluntary association in development programmes designed to provide direct benefits to them have now brought to surface the inadequacies of past approaches.

Contrary to earlier beliefs,[36] anthropological researches from a wide range of traditional societies have shown that tradition and modernity are not in conflict. Rather, they may be mutually reinforcing. 'The all too common practice of pitting tradition and modernity against each other as paired opposites tends to overlook the mixtures and blends which reality displays.'[37]

Traditional social and cultural patterns can well be utilised to promote the overall goals of development.[38] Farmers may be encouraged to adopt modern agricultural practices in the belief that from the resultant gains in additional incomes they will be better placed to meet their family and kinship obligations. The authority of the traditionally respected leaders can be invoked in aid of many development programmes at the village level. Summing up his experiences in the Middle East and North Africa, Jurgen von Muralt says:

> One of the most important policy questions in the introduction of social change and development at the local level is the problem of how traditional values and institutions can be harnessed to the purpose of development. The problem is to identify more precisely those practices, values and institutions that can be used for constructive social change, together with the strategies appropriate to different kinds of situations, and to incorporate this knowledge in specific programmes of development. Popular participation in development is facilitated where there is a strong

tradition of local organization. This is especially true since group action undoubtedly needs more than a perceived coincidence of individual self-interests; there must also be a certain sense of solidarity and mutual trust among the members of a group. When rational economic incentives can be successfully implanted in still functioning traditional associations, then there is a chance of transforming them into modern societies.[39]

The awareness that socio-cultural forces play a significant role, and that their neglect will have an adverse effect on the outcome of all developmental activity is rapidly increasing. Reporting on the Nigerian experience, S K Taime Williams concludes:

... It is now becoming increasingly clear that possession of technical knowledge alone is not enough in getting agricultural development moving on its path of contributing to overall economic development. This has to be buttressed with knowledge of some of the sociological factors such as land tenure system, family and village organizations, values and norms, systems of sanction and assignment of roles, and the role of strong solidarity among the people.[40]

The World Bank now clearly lays great stress on ensuring that tradition is kept on the right side of development and not allowed to take a back seat as has been the case so far. The World Bank Annual Report, 1980 says:

Lessons have also been learned from the better understanding of the fact that the intended beneficiaries of these projects are members of traditional societies that must be, and are, cautious in initiating changes. The lesson, of course, is that projects must be designed to be even more sensitive to local conditions, and that an understanding of social structures and local behavior patterns must be developed before the project preparation stage. And that even then, projects must remain flexible so that signals received during implementation can be responded to, so that institutional arrangements can be altered and technical deficiencies remedied, and so that any unexpected social response can be adjusted to.[41]

In working with the rural poor for their development, it is of crucial significance that the concerned personnel are aware of the special characteristics of the traditional village society. They can then work effectively with the people to produce the intended results.

What Can Anthropologists Do?

Many anthropologists lament that they are not getting a fair deal from others in the development world, and that the importance of what they have to offer is not fully appreciated. Typical of such instances is a recent paper by Frank Roberto Vivelo which discusses his disillusionment with working in a multi-disciplinary team.[42] In an introductory note to this paper, M G Trend has made the following remarks:

...The author raises (and tries to deal with) some important questions concerning anthropology's fit in the world of contract research, where the territory has been defined by other disciplines, where the research sometimes seems narrowly conceived and unprudently normative, and where our discipline's greatest contribution seems to be the use of a method (field observation), rather than any unique anthropological perspective or theory. At its stereotypical worst, anthropology is perceived as mere ethnographic wool gathering practised by fuzzy thinkers who have an aversion to mathematics, and who incline toward producing 600-page ethnographies, rather than concise, actionable sets of policy recommendations based on objective procedures that allow replication and, hence, produce reliable results.[43]

If anthropologists think that they are being excluded from participation in decision-making and action in the field of development they cannot blame anybody else except themselves. Traditional village societies in the Third World, which are currently the focus of major development efforts, have all along been the subject of exclusive professional interest to anthropologists. The knowledge concerning the poor which anthropology has built up over the years should therefore be critically important to rural development.[44] Unfortunately, anthropologists themselves have not given enough thought to working for rural development. M N Srinivas writes

While social anthropologists have carried out village studies, they have fought shy of writing on rural development. This is indeed a pity for they have acquired, as a result of their painstaking studies, intimate and accurate knowledge of rural culture, and built into social anthropological research is an approach which is productive of insights into the nature of the relationships obtaining between different aspects of rural social life and culture. Unfortunately, however, they are not being used for promoting rural development.[45]

There is nothing in the field of anthropology which makes any aspect of it irrelevant to development, kinship studies included. Reporting on Ghana, Janice Jiggins recently noted:

West Africa generally and Ghana in particular is the _locus classicus_ of British social anthropological kinship studies, a subject many development specialists would regard as an arcane academic matter of little relevance to development policy and practice. I would argue, on the contrary, that understanding patterns of family relationship and inheritance — what has been called the domestic domain — is necessary, and practically relevant to development practitioners.[46]

However, to be useful as members of interdisciplinary development teams, anthropologists need to be better equipped. They should be familiar with the issues in development, the methods of administration, the role of other disciplines, etc. As Glynn Cochrane has shown, anthropologists are frequently not equipped to play their part as development experts.[47] Development agencies do require the services of anthropologists, but not of the kind which universities have traditionally been producing.

Reluctance on the part of anthropologists to come out openly to assist rural development, and to adapt teaching on the campuses to the requirements of development agencies explains why anthropologists have little experience of rural development administration. When they do get opportunities to work, they are unable to contribute much because of any previous background.[48] On assignments to evaluate the projects (not an easy task in the best of circumstances) anthropologists, usually without sufficient prior experience of governmental agencies to be able to tell what sort of criticism would be acceptable and influential in future plans, have been found to be merely critical.[49]

The fact is that anthropologists are in demand, and their contribution is openly acknowledged. The Annual Report of the World Bank for 1977 is quite explicit in this connection:

> Greater understanding is needed of the social and cultural constraints affecting the rural poor. Often, the chronically poor have fallen into behavioural patterns and attitudes which tend to prevent them from taking full advantage of their own development potential. To gain a better understanding of the pathology of poverty, the Bank, in several cases, is now including sociological and anthropological assessments as part of project design and appraisal.[50]

What is the nature of the distinctive anthropological contribution to development? In a recent article Mandelbaum has outlined special resources of anthropology:[51]

1. *Holistic view*: An important lesson of anthropology is to view man in his totality. The insistence on seeing the whole, interconnections among parts, etc., has enabled anthropologists to gain insights into traditional societies which otherwise is not possible.
2. *Field-work*: Anthropology has a long tradition of field-work in villages across the Third World. It is mainly through the participant observation technique that anthropologists obtain data and other information for their writings. Living among the people in remote villages, they acquire knowledge of such details which is not possible to obtain through any other research method.[52]
3. *Relating Microview to Macroview*: With their knowledge of local conditions as also the wider national culture, anthropologists are in a unique position to relate the microview to the macroview.
4. *Comparative Perspective*: Often studies done by anthropologists in a comparative frame cover a wide range of societies. In an increasingly interdependent world, most problems acquire a global dimension. A comparative perspective emerging from anthropological studies can be useful.

In order to view the anthropological contribution in a proper perspective, it would be helpful to be aware of its weaknesses as well. Some of the criticism levelled against anthropological methods particularly must be noted. Adian Southall has criticised the holistic approach of anthropology. The argument runs as follows:

... One reason why anthropology cuts little ice is because it insists on the whole and the general in an age devoted to specialization. It is all right, simply because not very relevant or important, for anthropologists to attempt the study of remote and small-scale socio-cultural systems as wholes, but when large-scale and modern situations are studied, anthropology must surely give way to the more precise, narrow, specialised disciplines; to economics, sociology, political science, and, indeed, the new subspecializations to which even they give place: econometrics, public administration, regional science, and the rest.[53]

Field-work which is the hallmark of anthropology has also come under fire recently. Michael Barkun has criticised it: '... the field-work dogma has increasingly made social anthropology the victim of its virtues. An insistence upon the particular and the concrete makes comparison appear both unattractive and unprofitable. For any generalization can be demolished by recourse to a single contrary ethnographic report.'[54]

In a generally critical way, Glynn Cochrane suggests that anthropology still has a long way to go before its conclusions can be acceptable to development agencies:

... Different economists will be able, independently, to arrive at the conclusion that there will be roughly similar rates of return on an economic investment project. But will several anthropologists give the same advice, if consulted, about a particular investment project? I suspect that most potential users of anthropology think the answer is 'no', intuitively sensing that the cherished individualism of the anthropologist is at variance with the degree of uniformity of judgment and predictability that characterize the objectivity and verifiability of professional statements. Anthropology needs to convince potential users of the discipline that it can be a profession whose members can be relied on to perform with the degree of uniformity and reliability associated with engineers, doctors and lawyers.[55]

The value of anthropological studies of village communities for purposes of national planning is often debated. A question that constantly arises is: How can such studies be used to make nation-wide plans of development? On the basis of his study of two Indonesian towns, Clifford Geertz observes:

> In the main, the value of systematic studies of particular communities for the understanding of the national economic development lies (1) in their more intensive probing of particular dynamics which are, nevertheless, of broader general significance; and (2) in their more circumstantial depiction of the nature of the social and cultural context within which development inevitably will have to take place.[56]

As a basis of prediction, T Scarlett Epstein believes that studies by anthropologists offer a more sound basis than do many of the unreliable macro-economic surveys in the developing countries. Macro-predictions require statistical data of a sophistication which is often unavailable. But the limitations of micro-predictions are not inconsiderable, she admits:

> There is, for example, the question of 'representativeness' and the problems of generalizing from a situation in which there can be no guarantee that all the relevant variables are present. There is the further and related issue that the more restricted the form of observation, the greater the likelihood of the local situation under study being affected by intrusive factors.[57]

Ideally, the macro-approach of the economist and the micro-approach of the anthropologist must be combined if planning is to be more realistic.[58] Anthropologists will also need to modify some of their time-consuming field-work methods to be able to assist planners at a short notice.[59] Consideration should also be given to change the method of village studies so that their generalisations are valid for the region, if not for the whole country. A single village study can be supplemented by visits to a number of villages in the region to gain first-hand knowledge of relevant developments.

At present accurate, intimate knowledge of the people and their culture acquired through the field-work method remains the main strength of anthropology. This knowledge is directly relevant to rural development planning and operations.[60] Though anthropological theory and methods are still in their own developmental stage, the insights of anthropologists can nevertheless contribute significantly to overall development planning and administration. As Everett M Rogers and Nat J Colletta observe, this can be done

By identifying, through structured interest-group and class analysis, precisely who stands to gain or to lose in a community by supporting a given human development effort. Equally significantly, such researchers can uncover motivational resources and behavioral dispositions, patterns of loyalty, and deeply rooted cultural values. These values can act as constraints, or they can be mobilized and supported through educational efforts to facilitate the goals of human development programs geared to the reduction of poverty.[61]

Commenting on the uniquely anthropological contribution to development, Glynn Cochrane emphatically states:

The Third World badly needs the kinds of expertise that only anthropologists possess. What special attributes does anthropology have? What would be the utility of an anthropological dimension in development work? My own experience suggests some obvious strengths: first, anthropological methods of data collection are capable of producing unique information of high quality; second, anthropologists have an interest in human motivation which is of inestimable value in making calculations about development policies and their consequences; third, anthropologists have a humanistic orientation which usually causes them to examine the ethical and moral basis for change against the needs of the people whose wants those changes are supposed to serve.[62]

Development experience during the past quarter century has firmly established the value of socio-cultural factors in the development process. Increasingly, it is being recognised that the constraints to rural development have much to do with an inadequate understanding of the people experiencing change. Anthropologists are getting more and móre opportunities to work for development agencies, both national and international. This seems to be a good beginning.

On rural development projects huge sums of money have come to be invested in recent years. In future this investment trend is expected to gain further momentum. It is, therefore, extremely important that improvements are now quickly perceptible in the income levels of the poorer groups. Indeed it would be a human failure of the worst kind, and not just some financial loss, if the poor cannot be helped to develop only because of the planners' ignorance about their lifestyle.

NOTES AND REFERENCES

1. A popular account of poverty in the Third World may be seen in Paul Harrison. 1981. *Inside the Third World*. Harmondsworth: Penguin Books. Another popular work on the subject of world development is Geoffrey Lean. 1978. *Rich World, Poor World*. London: George Allen and Unwin.
2. *World Development Report, 1980*. Washington DC: The World Bank. August 1980. Pp. 33-34.
3. Robert S. McNamara. 1978. Foreword. *World Development Report, 1978*. August 1978. P. iii.
4. Jonathan Power and Anne-Marie Holstein. 1980. *World of Hunger: A Strategy for Survival*. New Delhi: Heritage Publishers. P. 8.
5. See in this connection, Robert Chambers. 1980. *Rural Poverty Unperceived: Problems and Remedies*. Washington DC: The World Bank (World Bank Staff Working Paper No. 400).
6. *North-South: A Programme for Survival*. The Report of the Independent Commission on International Development Issues under the Chairmanship of Willy Brandt. London: Pan Books. 1980. P. 49.
7. A popular account of the current development efforts undertaken to alleviate poverty is available in Paul Harrison. 1980. *The Third World Tomorrow*. Harmondsworth: Penguin Books Ltd.
8. *Rural Development: Sector Policy Paper*. Washington DC: The World Bank. February 1975. P. 3.
9. Mahbub ul Haq. 1976. *The Poverty Curtain: Choices for the Third World*. New York: Columbia University Press.
10. *Rural Development* (Evaluation Study No. 2). New York: United Nations Development Programme. June 1979.

11. Irma Adelman and Cynthia Taft Morris. 1973. *Economic Growth and Social Equity in Developing Countries.* Stanford: Stanford University Press. P. 192.

12. *Poverty and Landlessness in Rural Asia.* Geneva: International Labour Office. 1977.

13. Ozay Mehmet. 1978. *Economic Planning and Social Justice in Developing Countries.* London: Croom Helm.

14. Glynn Cochrane. 1979. *The Cultural Appraisal of Development Projects.* New York: Praeger Publishers.

15. *Sector Paper on Agriculture and Rural Development* (A Bank Staff Working Paper). Manila: Asian Development Bank.

16. Paul G. Hiebert. Anthropology and Programs of Village Development: A South Indian Case Study. *In* Robert Eric Frykenberg (ed.). 1977. *Land Tenure and Peasant in South Asia.* New Delhi: Orient Longman. Pp. 161-81.

17. William C. Thiesenhusen. Reaching the Rural Poor and Poorest: A Goal Unmet. *In* Howard Newby (ed.). 1978. *International Perspectives in Rural Sociology.* Chichester: John Wiley & Sons. Pp. 159-82.

18. Milton J. Easman and John D. Montgomery. The Administration of Human Development. *In* Peter T. Knight (ed.). 1980. *Implementing Programs of Human Development.* Washington DC: The World Bank (World Bank Staff Working Paper No. 403).

19. Cora Du Bois. 1959. *Social Change in Southeast Asia.* Cambridge, Mass: Harvard University Press. Cora Du Bois observes: 'The reason for a failure to be practical may lie in the fact that anthropology still possesses no serious and generally acceptable theoretical structure. Cultural studies are still in need of their Einstein, their Darwin, or their Mendel....'

20. Asian Development Bank. 1977. *Rural Asia: Challenge and Opportunity.* Singapore: Federal Publications. P. 220.

21. Charles A. Murray. *Investment and Tithing in Thai Villages: A Behavioral Study of Rural Modernization.* Unpublished doctoral dissertation, Massachusetts Institute of Technology. 1974. Quoted here from Robert E. Krug *et al.* Measuring Village Commitment to Development. *In* Harold Lasswell, Daniel Lerner and John D. Montgomery (eds.). 1976. *Values and Development: Appraising Asian Experience.* Cambridge, Mass: The MIT Press.

22. Hari Mohan Mathur. Ending Poverty, Unemployment and Inequality: Experience and Strategy, *Development Policy and Administration Review,* Vol. 1, No. 2, July-December 1975, p. 7.

23. Warren L. Prawl. It's the Agents of Change Who Don't Like Change. *CERES: FAO Review,* Vol. 2, No. 4, July-August 1969.

24. S.H. Alatas. 1976. *The Myth of the Lazy Native.* London: Frank Cass.

25. W.F. Wertheim. Resistance to Change — From Whom? *In* Hans-Dieter Evers (ed.). 1973. *Modernization in South-East Asia.* Kuala Lumpur: Oxford University Press.

26. *World Development Report, 1980.* Washington DC: The World Bank. P. 76.

27. On what should be done to strengthen development administration so that it becomes an effective instrument of service to the rural poor see, Alec McCallum. Unsnarling the Bureaucracy: Devolution and Rural Development. *CERES,* Vol. 13, No. 2, March-April 1980.

28. Oscar Lewis. 1967. *La Vida.* London: Secker and Warburg. The Culture of

Poverty as discussed by Oscar Lewis in this work has tended to create an impression that culture is a deterministic factor in sustaining poverty. See, L. Richard Della Fave. The Culture of Poverty Revisited: A Strategy for Research. *Social Problems,* Vol. 21, No. 5, June 1974, pp. 609-20. Also see, Barbara E. Coward *et al.* The Culture of Poverty Debate: Some Additional Data. In the same issue of *Social Problems,* pp. 621-33.

29. Goran Djurfeldt and Staffan Linberg. 1975. *Behind Poverty: The Social Formation in a Tamil Village.* Lund: Studentlitteratur.
30. Stanley J. Heginbotham. 1975. *Cultures in Conflict: The Four Faces of Indian Bureaucracy.* New York: Columbia University Press. This study shows how completely the bureaucracy of development parallels the old pre-independence set-up.
31. F.G. Bailey. 1957. *Caste and the Economic Frontier: A Village in Highland Orissa.* Manchester: Manchester University Press. Pp. 249, 253.
32. Joan P. Mencher. Family Planning in India: The Role of Class Values. *Family Planning Perspectives,* Vol. 2, No. 2, March 1970, p. 38.
33. S.C. Dube. 1958. *India's Changing Villages.* London: Routledge and Kegan Paul Ltd. P. 138.
34. John P. Powelson. Why Are the Poor So Poor in Less Developed Countries. *Human Organization,* Vol. 34, No. 1, Spring 1975, p. 101.
35. J.D.Y. Peel. Olaju: A Yoruba Concept of Development. *The Journal of Development Studies,* Vol. 14, No. 2, January 1978, pp. 139-65.
36. Daniel Lerner. 1958. *The Passing of Traditional Society: Modernization in the Middle East.* Glencoe, Ill.: Free Press.
37. W.W. Ogionwo. The Adoption of Technological Innovations in Nigeria: A Study of Factors Associated with Adoption of Farm Practices. Doctoral dissertation. University of Leeds. 1969. Quoted here from J.E. Goldthorpe. 1975. *The Sociology of the Third World.* Cambridge: Cambridge University Press. P. 222.
38. It must be admitted that there are features in the traditional society that do come in the way of ready acceptance of innovations. Societies differ, and they are at different stages of 'modernisation'.
39. Jurgen von Muralt. Rural Institutions and Planned Change in the Middle East and North Africa. *In* Orlando Fals Borda and Inayatullah (eds.). 1969. *A Review of Rural Cooperation in Developing Areas.* Vol. I. Geneva: UNRISD.
40. S.K. Taime Williams. Getting Local Traditions on Your Side. *CERES: FAO Review,* Vol. 4, No. 2, March-April 1971.
41. *World Bank Annual Report, 1980.* Washington DC: The World Bank. P. 29.
42. Frank Roberto Vivelo. Anthropology, Applied Research, and Nonacademic Careers: Observations and Recommendations with a Personal Case History. *Human Organization,* Vol. 3, No. 4, Winter 1980, pp. 345-57.
43. M.G. Trend. Introductory Notes to a Cautionary Tale. *Human Organization,* Vol. 39, No. 4, Winter 1980, p. 344.
44. Hari Mohan Mathur. Preface. *In* Hari Mohan Mathur (ed.). 1977. *Anthropology in the Development Process.* New Delhi: Vikas Publishing Co.
45. M.N. Srinivas. Reflections on Rural Development. *Kurukshetra: India's Journal of Rural Development,* Vol. XXVII, No. 18, 16 June 1979, p. 11. This article by M.N. Srinivas is a slightly amended version of the Dr. Vikram Sarabhai Memorial Lecture for 1978, delivered at Ahmedabad on 28 March 1979.

46. Janice Jiggins. 1978. *Report on Ghana*. London: Overseas Development Institute. (AAU 2/78). P. 20.
47. Glynn Cochrane. 1971. *Development Anthropology*. New York: Oxford University Press.
48. On a related theme of the relationship between anthropologists and administrators see, J. Ingersoll. Anthropologists and the Agency for International Development (AID): An Old Hate Relationship and a New Love Affair. *Anthropological Quarterly*, Vol. 50, No. 4, October 1977.
49. The Role of the Social Sciences in Rural Development. An Inter-Agency Conference, 1975. New York: The Rockefeller Foundation. 1976. P. 16.
50. *World Bank Annual Report, 1977*. Washington DC: The World Bank. P. 12.
51. David G. Mandelbaum. Anthropology and Challenges of Development. *Economic and Political Weekly*, Vol. XV, No. 44, 1 November 1980, pp. 1898-1901.
52. Other disciplines also are now becoming increasingly involved in village studies. See, Biplap Dasgupta (ed.). 1978. *Village Studies in the Third World*. Delhi: Hindustan Publishing Corporation (India). Of interest in this volume is the paper by G. Parthasarthy, Indian Village Studies and the Village Poor. Pp. 149-64.
53. Adian Southall. Community, Society, and the World in Emergent Africa. *In* Manfred Stanley (ed.). 1972. *Social Development: Critical Perspectives*. New York: Basic Books
54. Michael Barkun. Anthropology, Change and the Social Sciences. *In* Stuart S. Nagel (ed.). 1975. *Policy Studies and the Social Sciences*. Lexington, Mass: DC Heath and Company. P. 152.
55. Glynn Cochrane. Introduction. *In* Glynn Cochrane (ed.). 1976. *What We Can Do For Each Other: An Interdisciplinary Approach to Development Anthropology*. Amsterdam: B.R. Gruner Publishing Co. P. 4.
56. Clifford Geertz. 1963. *Pedlars and Princes*. Chicago: The University of Chicago Press. P. 142.
57. T. Scarlett Epstein. The Role of Social Anthropology in Development Studies. *In* Hari Mohan Mathur (ed.). 1977. *Anthropology in the Development Process*. New Delhi: Vikas Publishing House. P. 100.
58. See in this connection, T. Scarlett Epstein. 1975. The Ideal Marriage Between the Economist's Macroapproach and the Social Anthropologist's Microapproach to Development. *Economic Development and Cultural Change*, Vol. 24, No. 1, October.
59. For some comments on saving time on the field-work by use of appropriate techniques see, Comments by Hari Mohan Mathur on the paper by Marilyn Gates. Measuring Peasant Attitudes to Modernization: A Projective Method *Current Anthropology*, Vol. 17, No. 4, December 1976, p. 660.
60. Allen D. Jedlicka. 1977. *Organization for Rural Development: Risk-Taking and Appropriate Technology*. New York: Praeger Publishers. Pp. 24-27.
61. Everett M. Rogers and Nat J. Colletta. Social and Cultural Influences on Human Development Policies and Programs. *In* Peter T. Knight (ed.). 1980. *Implementing Programs of Human Development*. Washington DC: The World Bank (World Bank Staff Working Paper No. 403). P. 297.
62. Glynn Cochrane. Preface. *In* Glynn Cochrane (ed.). 1976. *What We Can Do For Each Other: An Interdisciplinary Approach to Development Anthropology*. Amsterdam: B.R. Gruner Publishing Co. P. ix.

Ending Poverty, Unemployment and Inequality

Evidence accumulating from recent studies of the way development has worked in the last quarter century lends support to the widely held view that faster economic growth does not inevitably lead to an improvement in the condition of the poor.[1] Undeniably, the rate of growth in this period has been fairly high—higher than at any time before. But often the benefits of growth have been inequitably distributed, and as a result the misery of the poor has failed to diminish and in many cases has actually increased. Michael Lipton has noted:

> Most poor countries have in the past quarter century enjoyed unprecedented growth of income per person; substantial 'development' as measured by the per caput availability of doctors and teachers, roads and electricity, steel and fertilizers; but nevertheless, little or no improvement in the living standards of the worst-off 40-50 per cent of the people, certainly in the countryside, possibly even in urban areas.[2]

Contrary to what planners had anticipated at the time the development process began, the fruits of planned growth have not trickled down to the poorest. On the basis of a study analysing data from 74 developing countries Adelman and Morris even go as far as stating categorically that 'hundreds of millions of desperately poor people throughout the world have been hurt rather than helped by economic development.'[3]

By 1965 doubts were being expressed that economic growth, howsoever essential, might not by itself solve or even alleviate the problems of poverty within a foreseeable future. The basic premise of planners that sustained high growth rate automatically leads to higher real incomes for even the poorest is now increasingly being questioned. Today planners are no longer assuming — as they did in the 1950s and the early 1960s — that increases in the per capita GNP would in the end automatically trickle down to the poorest and that their job should be to merely continue accelerating the pace of economic growth rate. Even the validity of the GNP as an indicator of overall development is now disputed. In fact many scholars think that development could better be measured by some other indicators and that exclusive reliance on the GNP will only give a distorted picture. Dudley Seers is of the view that

> The questions to ask about a country's development are therefore: What has been happening to poverty? What has been happening to unemployment? What has been happening to inequality? If all these three become less severe, then beyond doubt this has been a period of development for the country concerned. If one or two of these central problems have been growing worse, especially if all three have, it would be strange to call the result 'development', even if per capita income had soared.... A 'plan' which conveys no targets for reducing poverty, unemployment and inequality can hardly be considered a 'development plan'.[4]

Poverty, unemployment and inequality have always persisted, but the fact that these should tend to increase rather than decrease in the wake of development effort is surely a cause for great concern everywhere. It would be worthwhile to examine the efforts made in the past to end poverty, unemployment and inequality and to consider policy instruments that may now help in achieving success in this endeavour.

Past Development Experience

What has happened to poverty, unemployment and inequality in India? To what extent have the earlier development efforts mitigated them? It is necessary to understand the past development experience in order that an effective strategy to attack these problems is fashioned.

Considerable data have now been accumulated on the distribution of gains from development to various sections of the Indian society.[5] It is generally agreed that the achievements of planning in India have not been inconsiderable. However, the share of the poor in the progress has been minimal. It is the well-to-do who have benefited most from the development process. The income and consumption levels of the rich stand in sharp contrast with those of the poor. Dandekar and Rath conclude from their study of poverty in India:

The gains of development have remained largely confined to the upper middle and richer sections constituting 40 per cent of the population. While the overall per capita consumption increased by about 3-9 per cent in seven years, the consumption of the upper 40 per cent of the rural population increased by at least 44 per cent and that of the 40 per cent of the urban population increased by at least 4-8 per cent. These increases are not extraordinary and they are certainly not undesirable. Unfortunately they have remained largely confined to the upper middle and richer sections of the population. The middle, lower middle and poorest sections of the rural population showed much smaller increases in their per capita consumption and the per capita consumption of the poorest 5 per cent actually declined a little. The situation in urban areas appears even more serious. The per capita consumption of the lower and middle and poorer sections constituting 40 per cent of the urban population declined and the consumption of the poorest 10 per cent declined by as much as 15 to 20 per cent. Such unequal distribution of the gains of development inevitably leads to growing inequality and widening [the] gulf between the rich and the poor.[6]

Other studies have also reached similar conclusions. Robert S McNamara has summed up this growth and poverty situation in the following words:

In India, there has been progress in overall GNP growth during the past decade. But today some 40 per cent of the entire population — 200 million people — live at a level below the poverty line, a level at which serious malnutrition begins. The poorest 10 per cent of the nation — 50 million people — have not only not shared in the progress of the decade but may even have grown poorer.[7]

Why should have development led to an accentuation of disparities and worsening of the lot of the poor? Was planning done only to help the rich? What, in fact, has been the policy towards the poor? These are some of the questions that naturally arise when one looks at the pattern of past development which all along has benefited not those who were most in need but those who were already better off.

Concern for welfare of the poor has always been the explicitly stated objective of planners in India. The First Five-Year Plan clearly stated:

> Planning even in the initial stages should not be confined to stimulating economic activity within the existing social and economic framework. That framework itself has to be remoulded so as to ensure progressively for all members of the community full employment, education, security against sickness and other disabilities and adequate income.[8]

Subsequent plans have reiterated these egalitarian objectives in more emphatic language.

This egalitarian concern is clearly reflected in the laws enacted and the programmes launched to ensure that the poor participate actively in the mainstream of national life. For the rural poor, laws to reform tenurial arrangements and to redistribute land were enacted. Various labour and other laws were also enacted with the urban poor in view. Programmes for welfare of the tribals and other poor groups were specially launched. Measures were initiated to ensure that economic power did not become concentrated in the hands of a few. Income and wealth tax rates were deliberately kept very high. Controls and several licensing procedures sought to ensure that industrial growth did not benefit only the advantaged entrepreneurs.

Further, the government was not content with merely laying down the broad policies. It kept a close watch on the impact of these policies on different segments of the population so that necessary corrective action could be taken in good time. As early as in 1960 the Committee on Distribution of Income and Levels of Living (1964) was set up to study gains from the development process to different groups of people, and speaking on this occasion the late Prime Minister Jawahar Lal Nehru observed:

> Again it is said that the national income over the First or Second Plan has gone up by 42 per cent and the per capita income by 20 per cent. Now a legitimate query is made where has this gone? It is a very legitimate query: to some extent of course, you can see where it has gone. I do sometimes address large gatherings in the villages and I can see that they are generally better-fed and better-clothed, they build brick houses and they are generally better. Nevertheless, that does not apply to everybody in India. Some people probably have hardly benefited. Some people may even be facing various difficulties. The fact remains, however, that this advance in our national income, in our per capita income, has taken place and I think it is desirable that we should enquire more deeply as to where this has gone and appoint some expert committee to enquire into how exactly this additional income that has come to the country or per capita has spread.[9]

Given the planner's slant towards the poor and the pursuit of an egalitarian development policy, what has been achieved till date does not measure up to the expectations that were initially aroused. T Scarlett Epstein who recently revisited two villages in Mysore after a period of nearly 15 years concludes on the basis of her micro-level study of these communities:

> If the experience of Wangala and Dalena is in any way representative of larger areas of rural India, then it is clear that planning has failed in one of its major objectives. I have shown that social inequality in these two villages has continued almost unchanged while economic differentiation has considerably increased during the last fifteen years: the poor have become poorer not only relatively but also absolutely.[10]

If it is not for not trying to improve the living conditions of the poor, what is it that really accounts, for the unmitigated persistence of poverty, unemployment and inequality in the face of growth that planned effort over the years has generated? Indeed, there is no simple answer to this question. But something perhaps can be learnt from examining the way the development process actually worked. This might yield some insights that planners may find useful in formulating more effective development strategies in future. On paper the broad policies that have been pursued over the years look the kind which should be able to promote egalitarian goals ideally. But, in fact, they could not all be implemented in the manner envisaged. Some policies made assumptions which were far removed from reality at the grassroots level. The case of land reforms will illustrate this point. Explaining reasons for the lack of success in this effort, Arun Shourie concludes that some of the assumptions of law-makers concerning the village society were not quite correct: '

> The expectation has been that the patterns of land ownership and operation can be transformed by passing laws in national and state capitals, by relying on itinerant officers to implement them and by making the reforms justiciable. In brief, the expectation has been that outsiders — the distant legislator, the itinerant officer, the scholarly judge — can transform the most important feature of village life, the ownership and operation of land. But how are such men to monitor every lease, to examine the precise relationship between each sharecropper and his landlord, to ascertain the extent to which each landlord actually tills his land? And how is a lowly tenant — who must continue to live in the village long after the officer has driven off; whose lease, in all probability, is an oral one; who is, most likely illiterate, weak and indebted to his landlord — to gather written evidence, muster witnesses and accuse his landlord in an open court that passes all the Western norms of justiciability?[11]

There were, then, too many exemption clauses in the laws and the landlords took full advantage of this to retain with themselves virtually all the land which they had come to possess. It would be difficult to argue that these laws benefited sharecroppers and poor tenants to the extent desired. The fact that so many amendments have recently been made to make these laws capable of more effective implementation can well be taken to mean that the earlier exemption clauses were purposely devised to perpetuate hold of the big landlords. If some of the earlier measures did not succeed in giving to the poor all that they had promised it should not come as a complete surprise.

Barring a few such laws which were deficient in some ways, there however, seems to be nothing to suggest that policies were designed specially to benefit the rich at the expense of the poor. It is the way these policies were implemented that actually led to only the rich profiting from development, leaving the poor in their pristine poverty.

On the failure of administrators to implement policies effectively enough has been written. Their inability to deliver benefits of development to the poor has been due to a number of factors. Administrators usually come from a background quite different from that of the poor — their education, interests, and lifestyle are quite different. And since administrators and citizens are separated by distinctions of all sorts, administrators are not in a position to understand the problems of the poor or do very much for them. Even on tours to villages, undertaken specifically to settle on the spot the problems of the poor, the district officers are not able to communicate directly with them. The poor do not approach them either. Instead, they try and approach the officials through intermediaries — Sarpanchas or other such village dignitaries — who see to it that this method of contact alone is followed. Often the district officers devote more of their time to attending on visiting senior administrators and VIPs from the capital. Most administrators then prefer the secretariat job as this keeps them closer to their senior colleagues, to the seat of power and authority. Work in the field is no longer valued as highly as before. The general situation in this regard which C,L,G, Bell describes rings true of the administrative scene in India:

> It is almost invariably the case that the able, diligent, or well-connected civil servant will spend much of his career in the company of his peers and politicians.... When he is posted to outlying towns or rural areas, usually early in his service, he may well regard the period spent there as necessary time-serving or as a punishment for falling out of favour, and chafe constantly to get back to the center. Thus, the active business of administration which is intimately bound up with implementing the strategy — agricultural and industrial extension, land reform, public works, and the like — is probably conducted by officers who are less gifted or disaffected or both. For in most countries, such work carries comparatively little prestige, and there is really no offsetting financial compensation — if anything, the reverse.[12]

There is a good deal of truth in the oft-repeated charge against the administrative system that it has not yet become completely development-oriented.

However, the failure of policies to achieve their stated egalitarian goal is not completely attributable to administrative shortcomings. A close look at the way these policies and programmes have actually worked would clearly show that at the local level there have been forces — deriving support from fairly high policy-making levels — which shaped the final outcome of the development effort. The rich in the village who wielded considerable influence at the decision-making level in government saw to it that whatever the policies might be they alone benefited from them to the extent possible. P K Bardhan has shown how various types of constraints on the effective implementation of good intentioned redistributive policies resulted in the inequitable distribution of gains from measures which had a definite egalitarian intent.[13]

It is common knowledge now that the rich through their influence have been making the most of public services like irrigation and electric supply which government operates for the benefit of all citizens. In command areas of the canal irrigation projects the influential farmers do all they can to ensure that their fields get maximum water at the time their fields require irrigation. They keep the officials of the irrigation department in good humour, complaining to the higher authorities against those officials who do not 'cooperate' with them.[14] In arid regions where water is a scarce commodity the affluent farmers are known to have used their influence in getting tube-wells located on their farmlands. In some cases the electric transmission lines were erected for distant villages not because this would have aided agricultural development but for reasons largely connected with the fact that some influential person happened to belong to those villages.

The poor do not know how to obtain any benefit from development programmes that in reality are meant to help them. Apart from the fact that they do not have securities to furnish for obtaining loans, the procedural difficulties in obtaining loans from credit agencies largely discourage them, instead they turn to local money-lenders who offer credit in a familiar, friendly way reducing lengthy paperwork to just putting a thumb-impression on a stamped sheet. Even when the poor are aware that the law is on their side, this knowledge does not always embolden them to approach the courts which follow dilatory procedures that simply are incapable of settling cases referred to them within any reasonable time limit. Litigation is, then, too expensive, far beyond the means of the poor.

When Panchayati Raj was introduced great hopes were aroused and it was expected that the Panchayats would be in a position to involve all the people in local efforts to build the village community along lines in which disparities would quickly vanish. But the people who were elected to the Panchayats and those who failed to get elected later ranged themselves into strong warring factions, usually along caste lines. Soon they became so busy in fighting amongst themselves — not always on issues relating to the improvement of the village life — that the task of development was simply relegated into the background. In fact this situation did not allow much development to occur, and where development did occur it only benefited the powerful and influential members of the Panchayat or their relatives and friends. The benefits did not trickle down to the poorest in the village.

In areas that experienced the 'Green Revolution' higher growth has only led to greater inequality. The big farmers were better placed than the small farmers to take advantage of the new technology, and they cashed in on this opportunity. With new technology the agricultural output was bound to increase substantially and in normal circumstances this would have lowered the food prices. But in order that big farmers were able to retain a comfortable profit margin, price support schemes were introduced, and there has been constant pressure in favour of keeping the price level as high as possible. In any case, the support prices have been much higher than those prevailing in the international market. All this has been done in the name of supporting innovations in agriculture. But the innovating farmers have not been content with just high prices assured for their product. They have been procuring inputs like seed, fertiliser, pesticide and agricultural machinery at low prices. This subsidy has further increased incomes of the 'progressive' farmers. Then, the proposals to directly tax agricultural income could not get far in the face of opposition from the influential farmers. It is the influence that the rich farmers are able to exert on the implementation of policies which, according to C H Hanumantha Rao, accounts for the growth of inequality in the countryside:

> Policies on land reform, credit and prices have been heavily biased towards big farmers who wield considerable political

power at the state level and who influence the formulation as well as implementation of such policies. Unlike the zamindars and the jagirdars, these rich farmers are rooted in the villages and display considerable drive for modern farming. They wield considerable influence over the peasantry and constitute the social base and 'vote banks' for the ruling party as well as for many of the opposition parties. They neither have the political courage nor feel the need to openly oppose the Central leadership on several schemes of agrarian reform. They, in fact, 'support' some of these radical measures but see to it that they become infructuous in implementation. Agriculture being a state subject, they have been in a position to undermine, if not reject, measures which go against their interests and to mobilise state power and resources to subserve their interests.[15]

On the other hand, small farmers have been excluded from the 'Green Revolution'. As Keith Griffin says: 'Those farmers who already possess resources in the form of land, capital and knowledge are able to grasp the opportunities created by the 'Green Revolution', and further improve their position. But those who are landless and illiterate will tend to lag behind and perhaps become further impoverished.'[16]

Small farmers have been facing problems in obtaining credit, inputs, and technical knowledge. Their incomes have been falling. They have been forced to sell their lands and have become landless labourers. And when they swell the ranks of the landless labour force the wages tend to further decline. The decline in wages is also likely to result from a large-scale adoption of labour-saving innovations by the progressive farmers.

No one would be opposed to innovations, but measures certainly need to be taken to ensure that benefits that accrue from agricultural modernisation are shared equally by all. Unless institutional reforms accompany technological innovation, only the elites would reap benefits, and the broad economic advance would not occur. People who do not participate in the development process will become frustrated and tensions may build up. Cliffton R Wharton, Jr. cautions:

If only a small fraction of the rural population moves into the modern century while the bulk remains behind, or perhaps even goes backward, the situation will be highly explosive. For example, Tanjore district in Madras, India, has been one of the prized areas where the new high-yield varieties have been successfully promoted. Yet one day last December, 43 persons were killed in a clash there between the landlords and their landless workers who felt that they were not receiving their proper share of the increased prosperity brought by the Green Revolution.[17]

Again, there is apparently nothing to suggest that the policies were tilted in favour of the rich. Some laws enacted in pursuance of these policies however, did not incorporate the provisions which would have helped their implementation in the desired manner. On the whole, it is the way the policies were executed that actually led to widening the gulf between rich and poor. In the prevailing environment perhaps it would not have been possible to implement the policies in any other different manner. Administrators who chose to act strictly according to dictates of the law some times found themselves in great trouble. A Planning Commission report has noted: 'As a matter of fact there have been cases where administrators who tried to implement land reform laws honestly and efficiently were hastily transferred elsewhere.'[18] At local levels, the rich really have been in a very dominant position and their only concern has been to maximise profits for themselves from opportunities that development brings. Occasionally, they did talk of the poor but they have been too preoccupied with the business of augmenting their own riches and influence to do anything for their less fortunate brethern.

Poverty-Focused Development Strategies

Can something not be done now to mitigate poverty, unemployment and inequality? If the poor have not fully shared in the fruits of development so far, is there no hope for them? These are some of the questions that arise when one looks at what development has done to the poor especially in the past two decades. It is important that policy-makers now address themselves to these questions because as Hans Christoph Rieger puts it:

A population that sees no hope in the future for attaining minimal accepted nutritional standards, for itself or for the next generation, while the better off sections of society monopolize the gains of development, is likely to lose faith in the ability of the Indian system of democratic planning to bring about the development which it claims to strive for.[19]

The outlook, however, is not so bleak. It is entirely possible to bring about considerable improvement in the situation of the poor. But success in this endeavour would largely depend on the kind of development strategy which is designed and pursued.

Although several recent studies suggest that inequality follows growth, this need not be the case always. In some developing countries distribution has not worsened as a result of development: it has actually improved in some countries where corrective measures have been adopted. Hollis Chenery has observed: 'the bulk of the developing countries in which the poor have shared equitably in income growth — Israel, Yugoslavia, Taiwan, Korea, Sri Lanka, Costa Rica, Tanzania — consists of countries that have taken positive action to this end.'[20] Writing on the IBRD/IDS study Richard Jolly says that two conclusions which have clearly emerged from it are

> That a high rate of economic growth appears to have no adverse effect on relative equality, and that increases in the concentration of income are not inevitable, even in capitalist countries advancing from low levels of per capita income. These are important points, particularly because it is often argued that income must become more unequally distributed as poor countries get richer.[21]

It is clear that corrective measures can influence quite remarkably the outcome of development efforts in favour of poorer segments of the population.

What strategies will ensure that the poorest not only share in the progress but also contribute to it? Some authorities still recommend growth-oriented strategies, and their argument is that once high growth rate has been achieved redistribution would be an easy task. Others, disappointed by the benefits of growth not trickling down to the poorest, now suggest that the main task of planners should be to see that community wealth and assets are first equally distributed between different sections of society, and that the growth factor for the time being be relegated to the sidelines. Neither of these two extreme approaches can perhaps solve the enormous problems confronting this country. There has to be a combination of both — growth as well as redistribution. The findings of the IBRD/IDS study, as Richard Jolly notes, also point in this direction.

In essence, the IBRD/IDS exposition of RwG develops the following points:

1. Strategies which combine redistribution with growth are essential if poverty in Third World countries of low per capita income is to be rapidly eliminated. Neither growth nor redistribution alone will be sufficient.
2. Four dimensions of policy are involved, usually in combination, in RwG strategies:
   (a) accelerating GNP growth through raising savings and allocating resources more efficiently with benefits to all groups in society;
   (b) redistribution of existing assets;
   (c) asset redistribution by redirecting new investment into the creation of assets generating income for the poorest; and
   (d) transfer of income in support of consumption of the poorest.[22]

Concerning growth-oriented strategies enough has been said in the past and, hence, the following discussion is restricted to poverty-focused and equity-oriented development strategies that will raise income levels of the poorest segment of the population. This area of policy planning has, at present, engaged the attention of governments and scholars everywhere.[23]

Some of the components of an effective redistribution with growth strategy include the following:

Redistribution of Land: Since the highest concentration of poverty is in rural areas, the land reform laws need to be implemented speedily. These can be most powerful as a redistributive measure. But land reform needs to be seen in a broader perspective. It must not be seen to only include vesting ownership rights on to the tiller of the land and redistributing land rendered surplus by ceiling on land holdings. In fact, it is being increasingly realised now that there is not enough land for redistribution and that exclusive reliance on land reform cannot be expected to solve all the problems of the rural poor. B. S Minhas has suggested that rural works programme must be simultaneously undertaken.[24]

Land reform can be successful only if other measures in its support are taken. V, K, R V Rao lists some of these measures which must be

Concerned with seeing that (*i*) conditions of tenancy are so regulated as to provide the tenant with greater motivation to increase productivity and give him a larger share in the output, (*ii*) institutional and service facilities are created which will give effective access to inputs for the small farmers, (*iii*) arrangements are promoted for bringing together a number of small holdings into larger units for defined operational purposes and (*iv*) tenants are induced to form themselves into associations for protection of their interests.[25]

Nationalisation of Business Enterprises: One way to reducing concentration of wealth is direct intervention in the economic life by the government. The policy should be to ensure that public enterprises run efficiently, and more and more business is gradually covered by them. When the state owns the means of production and distribution the chances of wealth getting concentrated in the hands of a few private entrepreneurs recede completely.

While the nationalisation of business enterprises makes impossible the concentration of wealth in the hands of a few, it does not directly help all the extremely poor groups. It is the middle levels and the organised industrial labour which profit from it most.

Fiscal Policy Measures: Fiscal measures are capable of effectively bringing about a reduction in the income and wealth disparities. Both income and wealth tax should aim at ensuring that rich do not continue to amass wealth. The taxation structure can curb conspicuous consumption by taxing luxury goods and services. Savings for development can be generated by adopting appropriate taxation measures. It should be ensured that indirect taxes do not burden the middle and poorer sections.

Minimum Wage Policy: The minimum wage policy can do much to assure a decent living to the workers. At present the minimum wage laws seem to be benefiting only the organised labour in the industrial sector. The wage law for agricultural labour is, indeed, difficult to enforce. The wage policy, thus, benefits a minority of the labour force. To be able to provide general welfare the policy must aim to benefit both organised as well as unorganised labour.

Employment Programme: Since both unemployment and under-employment are the direct causes of poverty, there should be a well-planned effort to attack these problems on a high priority basis. In fact job creation must become a clear development objective in itself. B_1S_1 Minhas and Dandekar and Rath have suggested rural works programme as a sure measure of meeting the challenge of poverty in the countryside.[26] Works programme for urban areas must offer self-employment schemes to the educated unemployed. Suitable programmes can be designed for both rural and urban areas, such as construction of minor irrigation dams, drainage works, afforestation projects, highway maintenance, building of market roads, etc. This programme will generate employment not only for the rural poor, but also civil engineers and other technically qualified personnel as they would be needed to plan and execute these works. The works undertaken should not only be productive in nature, but should also utilise local materials. Any programme encouraging labour-intensive works is on the right side of dividing the gains of development equitably.

Public Expenditure on Social Services: Frequently, governmental expenditure on education, health, transport, electrification, water supply and in other sectors ends by benefiting the already privileged few far more than the mass of the disadvantaged. It happens that better schools, better hospitals, better public transportation and other facilities are frequently located in areas where the rich live. Their access to decision-making levels in government helps them to ensure that they get most out of public expenditures. The poor usually get little or no comparable facilities. This expenditure, however, is of a productive nature, because it increases the capacity of the poor to produce more, and it increases their real incomes. It certainly helps reduce inequality. Policies relating to public expenditures therefore need to be reoriented so that the poor increasingly receive benefits from these services.

Welfare Programmes for the Weakest: Poverty amongst some tribal and other weaker sections of society is the most acute. These are groups that have lived on the periphery of the mainstream and have suffered neglect and exploitation. Special programmes should be launched for them. Before this is done, it is important that studies are conducted to identify the groups most in need of help. Such studies bringing out in detail the characteristics, composition, concentration, origin, habits, etc. of the poorer groups will aid the policy-making process. Sociologists and anthropologists should devote more attention to these problems. Unfortunately, not enough is known about the target groups, and about the methods that can really help them.

Choice of Technology: The highly sophisticated technology is capital-intensive. In a capital-short economy adoption of highly sophisticated technology results in employment of only a few workers and denial of job opportunity to many. While it is possible to distribute land, industrial capital cannot be redistributed. As Dandekar and Rath observe, the only method to distribute industrial capital more equitably is

To adopt a technology which would require less capital to employ a worker and hence, with given capital, would employ a larger number of workers. It is for this reason that the adoption of a labour-intensive technology is advocated. This certainly can be a method by which the small amount of capital that the economy has may be distributed among a large number of workers.[27]

If the objective is to minimise inequality and provide employment to more and more people for improving the income distribution, the policy should favour not the highly sophisticated technology but technology of the intermediate type.

Price Policy: Inflation erodes the real incomes of the masses, increases profit margins of the producers and distributors, and accentuates income inequalities. Stabilisation of the price level should, therefore, be a matter of highest concern to policy-makers. Several things can be attempted in this direction. By improving the public distribution system the benefits of subsidies on food and other essential commodities can be canalised towards poorer segments of the population. The dual pricing strategy has a great potential for inequality reduction.

Population Control Programme: The poorer groups still do not have easy access to family planning know-how and facilities. Consequently, they continue to reproduce at an alarmingly high rate. The rapid rise in their population is accentuating the maldistribution of income. Population explosion not only wipes out the progress achieved through the process of planned development, but also reduces availability per person of resources for the job creation.[28] Therefore, unless something drastic is done to limit the family size — by compulsion if necessary — no development strategy will be able to produce any significant impact on the incomes and levels of living of the poor.

None of these policies or programmes pursued in isolation will, however, improve income distribution and mitigate poverty and unemployment. It is only when these are pursued simultaneously as a package that both growth and equity will occur.

Most observers of the economic scene would agree that while the past development effort did succeed in raising the per capita income, its failure to ensure an equitable distribution of gains from the high growth rate has only meant greater misery to the poor who constitute roughly 40 per cent of the total population. And the unfortunate thing is that it is these policies and programmes designed ostensibly to further welfare of the poor that have led to this situation. To quote Adelman and Morris again:

> Development policies that ought in principle to have made for a more equitable distribution of income have served mainly as additional instruments for increasing the wealth and power of existing elites. Even more serious, new elites, many of whom owe their power to development programmes, have become adept at manipulating economic and political institutions to serve their private ends.[29]

Development planners and administrators can no longer neglect the poor. The poor cannot be expected to wait any further for development to produce the promised results for them. They must have now and here whatever development has to offer them.

The important question now is: What can be done to ensure that the process of planned development begins assisting the poor? Apparently, the existing development policies and the methods of execution require re-orientation. Henceforth policy-makers must focus on the question: Who benefits? It is only when beneficiaries happen to be the poor that new development programmes should be undertaken. Also, in the execution of these programmes the active participation of the poor must be invariably enlisted. In short, development planning must concern itself now with questions not only of economic growth but also with questions of social equity. Highly desirable, the two goals can be pursued together at the same time.

NOTES AND REFERENCES

1. See the following, Irma Adelman and Cynthia Taft Morris. 1973. *Economic Growth and Social Equity in Developing Countries.* Stanford University Press. Robert S. McNamara. 1973. *Address to the Board of Governors* (at Nairobi). Washington DC: International Bank for Reconstruction and Development. Hollis Chenery, Montek Ahluwalia *et al.* 1974. *Redistribution with Growth.* London: Oxford University Press. T. N. Srinivasan and P. K. Bardhan. 1974. *Poverty and Income Distribution in India.* Calcutta: Statistical Publishing Society.
2. Michael Lipton. 1974. Towards a Theory of Land Reforms. *In* David Lehmann (ed.). 1974. *Agrarian Reform and Agrarian Reformism.* London: Faber & Faber. P. 281.
3. Irma Adelman and Cynthia Taft Morris. 1973. P. 192.
4. Dudley Seers. 1972. What are We Trying to Measure? Reprinted from *The Journal of Development Studies,* Vol. 8, No. 3, April 1972. Brighton: Institute of Development Studies, IDS Reprints 106, p. 3.
5. V. M. Dandekar and Nilakantha Rath. 1971. *Poverty in India.* Poona: Indian School of Political Economy. Also see, P. K. Bardhan. 1973. *The Pattern of Income Distribution in India: A Review:* Paper prepared for the Development Research Centre of the World Bank. Washington DC (mimeographed). B.S. Minhas. 1970. *Planning and the Poor.* New Delhi: S. Chand and Co. NCAER. 1975. *Changes in Rural Income in India.* New Delhi: National Council of Applied Economic Research.
6. V. M. Dandekar and Nilakantha Rath. 1971. Pp. 30-31.
7. Robert S. McNamara. 1973. *One Hundred Countries, Two Billion People: The Dimensions of Development.* London: Pall Mall. P. 103.
8. Government of India. 1952. *First Five-Year Plan.* New Delhi: Planning Commission. P. 11.
9. Government of India. 1964. *Report of the Committee on Distribution of Income and Levels of Living, Part I — Distribution of Wealth and Concentration of Economic Power.* New Delhi: Planning Commission.
10. T. Scarlett Epstein. 1973. *South India: Yesterday, Today and Tomorrow.* London: Macmillan. P. 243.

11. Arun Shourie. 1973. Growth, Poverty and Inequalities. *Foreign Affairs*, Vol. 51, No. 2, January 1973, pp. 340-52; 344-45.
12. C. L. G. Bell. 1974. The Political Framework. *In* Hollis Chenery, Montek Ahluwalia *et al.* 1974. P. 68.
13. P. K. Bardhan. 1974. India. *In* Hollis Chenery, Montek Ahluwalia *et al.* 1974.
14. Daniel Thorner. 1962. The Weak and the Strong on the Sarda Canal. *In* Daniel Thorner and Alice Thorner (eds.). 1962: *Land and Labour in India.* Bombay: Asia Publishing House.
15. C. H. Hanumantha Rao. 1975. *Technological Change and Distribution of Gains in Indian Agriculture.* New Delhi: Macmillan. P. 186.
16. Keith Griffin. 1974. *The Political Economy of Agrarian Change: An Essay on the Green Revolution.* London: Macmillan. P. 212.
17. Cliffton R. Wharton Jr. 1969. The Green Revolution: Cornucopia or Pandora's Box? *Foreign Affairs*, 47(3), pp. 467-68.
18. Government of India. 1973. *Report of the Task Force on Agrarian Relations.* New Delhi: Planning Commission. P. 10.
19. Hans Christoph Rieger. 1975. Social and Economic Aspects of Economic Development Planning in India. *In* Peter Mayer (ed.). 1975. *Economic and Social Aspects of Indian Development.* Tubingen-Basel: Horst Erdmann Verlag. P. 105.
20. Hollis Chenery. 1974. Introduction. *In* Hollis Chenery, Montek Ahluwalia *et al.* 1974. P. xv.
21. Richard Jolly. 1975. Redistribution with Growth — A Reply. *IDS Bulletin*, Vol. 7, No. 2, August 1975, p. 10.
22. Richard Jolly. 1975. P. 11.
23. Gilbert Etienne. 1975. *The Overall Process of Rural Development: Economic Growth and Social Progress* (Occasional Paper No. 6). New Delhi: Training Division, Department of Personnel and Administrative Reforms, Cabinet Secretariat, Government of India.
24. B. S. Minhas. 1970. Rural Poverty, Land Redistribution and Development Strategy: Facts and Policy. *Indian Economic Review*, 5 (April), 97-1281.
25. V. K. R. V. Rao. 1974. *Growth with Justice in Asian Agriculture: An Exercise in Policy Formulation.* Geneva: UN Research Institute for Social Development.
26. B.S. Minhas. 1970; V.M. Dandekar and Nilakantha Rath. 1971.
27. V. M. Dandekar. 1971.
28. Robert Cassen. 1973. *Population, Development and the Distribution of Income* (IDS Communication 107). Brighton: Institute of Development Studies at the University of Sussex. Also see, T. Scarlett Epstein. 1975. Population Growth and its Social Dimension. *In* T. Scarlett Epstein and Durrell Jackson (eds.). 1975. *The Paradox of Poverty.* Delhi: Macmillan.
29. Irma Adelman and Cynthia Taft Morris. 1973. P. 201.

Index